Mix & Match **MAMA**
Eats

SHAY SHULL

HARVEST HOUSE PUBLISHERS
EUGENE, OREGON

Cover by Kyler Dougherty

Published in association with William K. Jensen Literary Agency, 119 Bampton Court, Eugene, Oregon 97404

Interior design Faceout Studio

Food photography by Shay Shull

All other photos by Claire McCormack Hogan

Mix-and-Match Mama Eats

Copyright © 2016 Mix and Match Mama

Published by Harvest House Publishers

Eugene, Oregon 97402

www.harvesthousepublishers.com

ISBN 978-0-7369-6613-9

ISBN 978-0-7369-6614-6 (eBook)

Printed in China

16 17 18 19 20 21 22 23 24 / DS / 10 9 8 7 6 5 4 3 2 1

For Andrew, Kensington, Smith, and Ashby

I am so blessed to sit at
our table each night and share a meal
with you. More than that,
I'm blessed to share my life with you.
Love you.

CONTENTS

INTRODUCTION

Maybe you picked up this book because you like to cook. Maybe you picked up this book because you read my blog. Maybe you picked up this book because you are tired of coming up with dinner ideas each night and you desperately need a few new tried-and-true recipes to turn to. You know what? Whichever gal you are, this book is for you!

Years ago, my girlfriend Rachel made us her chocolate chip Bundt cake one day for a little event. Well, we all just loved it and asked Rachel for the recipe. And after that...We all made this Bundt cake. We made it for every baby shower, church social, potluck, and dinner with friends. We made it so much that after a year, I just couldn't make or eat this cake again. That being said, I didn't want to try a new recipe. I loved her recipe. I love the simplicity, the easy directions, and the fact that it turned out every single time. I loved that method. So I took the method and tweaked it just a bit, mixing and matching it into a butterscotch Bundt cake. My girlfriends loved it! They loved it so much that the next time, I made it into a lemon Bundt cake, and then a pumpkin Bundt cake...and then Rachel finally asked me how many versions I thought I could make. I looked at her and blurted out the first number that came into my head...100.

Well, two years later, I finally finished my last Bundt cake in my little experiment, Bundt cake 101. Same recipe, same method, just with a few little tweaks.

I realized as I was making these cakes that women really want to serve a variety of foods to their families, but at the same time they want reliable, trustworthy, crowd pleasing recipes that they know will turn out each time. I took that philosophy and my love of mixing and matching and applied my concept to all food. Like sloppy joes? I can make 30 different versions using the same method. Monkey bread? Done! Burgers? Simple! Enchiladas, soups, casseroles, appetizers, breakfasts...you name it, I can mix and match it.

I want people to want to be in the kitchen. I want people to want to make yummy, seasonal, quick, and simple recipes for their families each day. More than anything, I want people to be sharing meals together. Sitting down at their tables, digging into hearty suppers, and pouring out their days to one another. That's what I want. I want togetherness for you and your family.

Food doesn't need to be complicated. Ingredient lists don't need to be long. Hours don't need to be spent slaving away over the stove. It should be quick. It should be simple. It should be seasonal. And it should be shared with the ones you love.

Unless noted, all entrée recipes in this book serve four.

From my kitchen to yours, happy cooking!

TIPS AND TRICKS

How to Get Cooked Chicken Quickly

1. Stick frozen or thawed chicken in a slow cooker on low 7 to 8 hours or high 3 to 4 hours with water (about 1 cup). This will poach your chicken, and then all you have to do is shred it with two forks right into your mixing bowl. Easy—and my favorite method!

2. Use a rotisserie chicken from the grocery store and shred that up.

3. Chop leftover grilled, baked, or sautéed chicken.

How to Make Slow Cooker Meals Taste Better

1. Always add something fresh at the end. Whether that's freshly grated cheese, chopped herbs, chopped green onion, or toasted nuts. Something fresh at the end always brightens up a slow-cooker meal.

2. Always brown your beef before you put it in the slow cooker. It only takes five extra minutes, but it helps your meal develop so much color and flavor.

My Best Entertaining Tips

1. Don't make all your own food! The Barefoot Contessa says that when hosting a party, you should make no more than three dishes yourself. Having a party is not about showing off how many recipes you can make. It's about being with your friends and family. It's about having fun! You need to take some help from the grocery store and buy dips, nuts, dessert, rolls, side dishes…whatever. Just let them help you! Don't overwhelm yourself by trying to make everything yourself. No one has fun with an anxious and busy host.

2. Candles! Candles! Candles! If you come to a party at my house, expect no less than twenty lit candles. I have them lit all over the place, even in rooms less frequented. It just says *party* when there are dim lights and candles.

3. Speaking of lights, dim yours! I hate going to a party where the main overhead lights are blaring. That seems so impersonal, like a doctor's office. Dim those lights, use lamps, and light your candles. Trust me, it will change the whole mood of the evening.

4. Listen to Michael Bublé. Okay, okay, you don't have to listen to Bublé (but you should!). Just have some sort of nice, relaxing music playing. Or have festive party music playing. The music really sets the tempo of the party.

5. **Don't cry.** You don't know how many times I've been to a party where the hostess has cried because some dish didn't turn out right. Calm down, take a deep breath, and laugh about it. Worst case scenario, you order a pizza. If you're stressed out, your guests will be too. Just laugh it off and have fun. I've been to some downer parties because the hostess was upset about her food.

6. **Keep it simple!** Casual food equals casual conversation. I love to serve big casseroles, taco bars, chili, and soups...you know, easy and relaxing food. My friend Lori is the total inspiration for this. Whenever I go to her house, she serves the best and yummiest food without fussing over it too much (soups and sandwiches, pasta salads, dips and chips). If you're fussing over Beef Wellington or Filet Mignon with Lobster Sauce, your guests will feel like it's a formal dinner, and they'll act stiff. I want them eating sloppy joes and feeling at ease at my house. Just because the mama cooks doesn't mean the mama needs to show off. A good old Tostada Bar with a festive dessert and some fun music will create the perfect party.

7. **It's the experience, not the food.** The sign of a good party? When I leave and don't really recall what I ate but remember the people, the easy conversation, and the warm feeling the home gave me. If I leave remembering every course I ate but didn't really engage with anyone, it wasn't a successful party. Cooking and entertaining are not the same thing. Focus on entertaining your guests and keep the food simple (order out if you need to!). Entertaining your guests and making sure they have the best time starts with your being relaxed...and if you're slaving over your stove, you aren't relaxed.

8. **Use white plates.** When you can, use white plates and serving platters. Food always looks better when served on white dishes. Mix and match them! They don't have to match. I like an eclectic table with an assortment of dishes. It makes everything seem more comfy and like home.

9. **Serve white drinks.** I love this tip! When you're hosting a party, serve white beverages. Whether it's a cocktail or mocktail...make it white. White beverages don't leave nasty stains like a punch or red cocktails. White drinks are a hostess's life-saver. Get creative—there are a lot of white drinks you can serve. I've served white hot chocolate, punches and mixed drinks with white bases, and white, fruity mixers (like lemonades, limeades, sherbets, etc.). Just do yourself a favor and make it white.

Baking Essentials

Everyone should keep these baking staples on hand!

1. A box of brownie mix.

2. A large box of instant vanilla pudding.

3. A box of yellow cake mix and a can of store bought chocolate frosting. A cake, cake balls, or cupcakes can be whipped up in no time with these two superstars.

4. A new bottle of cinnamon. I go through one bottle of cinnamon a month (seriously!) but I know most of you do not. Buy a new bottle every fall, so that your yummy fall food has maximum flavor. Old cinnamon in the cabinet will not taste the same as a fresh new bottle.

5. A new box of baking soda. I replace mine twice a year. You may or may not remember the last time you replaced yours. Go ahead and replace it today. A fresh box will not only help with your baking but freshen up your fridge as well.

6. A box of Baker's candy coating (white or dark chocolate). My friends make fun of me because I keep this stuff on hand and use it all the time to dip things in it (like pretzel rods, strawberries, cake balls, etc.). This stuff can help you out in no time if you need a last-minute dessert.

7. A new bottle of vanilla. Come on... When was the last time you bought one?

Grocery staples

The following items are always on my grocery list.

. . . .

PRODUCE DEPARTMENT
Berries
Apples
Lemons
Almonds
Onions
Garlic
Romaine lettuce
Spinach or kale
Basil
Fresh Parmesan cheese
Hummus
Bakery Bread
(and depending on the week, bell pepper, avocado,
tomatoes, bananas, oranges, green beans, etc.)

FROZEN FOODS DEPARTMENT
Cool Whip
Chopped spinach
Corn
(and depending on the week,
broccoli, puff pastry, etc.)

BAKING AISLE
Cake mix
Instant puddings
Chocolate chips
Butterscotch chips
Truvia
Flour
Sugar
Brown Sugar
Powdered Sugar
(and depending on the week,
Eagle Brand Milk, marshmallows, etc.)

MEAT DEPARTMENT
Lean ground beef
Chicken breasts (from behind the butcher's counter!)
(and depending on the week, turkey sausage,
ground turkey, brisket, salmon, etc.)

DAIRY DEPARTMENT
2% milk
OJ
Yogurt
Eggs
Butter
(and depending on the week, shredded cheeses,
cream cheese, sour cream, etc.)

"I never eat December snowflakes.
I always wait until January."

~LUCY, PEANUTS

JANUARY

DINNER

Buffalo Turkey Joes

Caramelized Onion Brisket Sliders

Mexican Calzones

Tex-Mex Sausage Corn Chowder

Beef and Ale Shepherd's Pie

White Chicken Chili

Stew

Mexican Meatloaf

Pizza Meatballs

Chicken and Dumplings

Spaghetti and Meat Sauce

Turkey and Spinach Lazy Lasagna

Chicken and Ranch Pasta

Mushroom Sausage Kale Pasta

Slow Cooker Stroganoff

BREAKFAST

Bacon and Tot Casserole

Oatmeal Four Ways

DESSERT

Butterfinger Blondies

Butterscotch Peach Cobbler

Chocolate Cinnamon
Bread Pudding

Vanilla Bean Poppy
Seed Cupcakes

Boston Cream Whoopie Pies

Mississippi Mud Bars

Buffalo Turkey Joes

All you buffalo wings people out there, rejoice! This is a sloppy joe that tastes like buffalo wings. The best part? They're simple and will be on your table in no time. Happy dinner!

INGREDIENTS

1 pound ground turkey

Few tablespoons extra virgin olive oil

Salt and pepper

1 (8 ounce) can tomato sauce

1 cup buffalo sauce

Burger buns

Chopped red onion, chopped green onion, chopped celery, and/or blue cheese to garnish

In a large skillet over medium-high heat, brown the ground turkey in a few tablespoons of olive oil. Sprinkle with salt and pepper. Once the turkey is browned and crumbly, reduce the heat to low and stir in tomato sauce and buffalo sauce. Let the sauce simmer just a few minutes.

Load one burger bun with turkey filling. Garnish with favorite buffalo toppings.

Caramelized Onion Brisket Sliders

Brisket is one of my favorite cuts of meat to throw in the slow cooker. It always turns out delicious and is so versatile. This is my basic brisket method that I just fancied up into little sliders. Because really, what's more fun on a busy weeknight than a slider supper?

INGREDIENTS

2 pound brisket (flat and trimmed)

1 (4 ounce) bottle of liquid smoke (use either hickory or mesquite flavored)

4 cups beef stock

Extra virgin olive oil

Salt and pepper

1 large onion, chopped

8 dinner rolls, split in half

4 ounces goat cheese

In a large pot over medium-high heat, brown both sides of your brisket in about two tablespoons of olive oil. Salt and pepper each side of the brisket quite liberally. After each side is browned (about 3 minutes per side) add brisket to slow cooker along with the entire bottle of liquid smoke and beef stock. Cover and cook on low about 8 hours or on high 4 hours.

Right before you're ready to serve, add your chopped onion to a large skillet over medium heat with a drizzle of olive oil and a big pinch of salt and pepper. Allow onion to sauté at least 10 minutes to get nice and caramelized.

When you're ready to assemble your sliders, remove brisket from slow cooker (discard all liquid) and slice up on your cutting board. Take each dinner roll and top with sliced brisket, a big scoop of caramelized onions and a dollop of goat cheese.

Mexican Calzones

A calzone that tastes like a taco? Sign my family up! All you need is a big green salad and dinner is done.

INGREDIENTS

1 (13 ounce) can refrigerated pizza dough (I use Pillsbury)

1 pound ground beef

1 (1 ounce) packet taco seasoning

2 cups salsa, plus a little more for garnish

1 (15 ounce) can chili beans

1 cup shredded Cheddar cheese

about 4 to 6 green onions, chopped to garnish

Extra virgin olive oil

Salt and pepper

Preheat oven to 425 degrees. Line a baking sheet with foil and spray with cooking spray (this will make cleanup a cinch!).

In a large skillet over medium-high heat, brown ground beef in a drizzle of olive oil until crumbly. Next, stir in taco seasoning, salsa, chili beans, and cheese. Reduce heat to low and simmer about five minutes.

Open the can of pizza dough and spread into a rectangle. Cut into four squares. On one half of each square, spread out a quarter of your taco meat mixture. Take the other half and fold on top. Press the sides down to seal all of your filling in. Then brush a drizzle of oil across the top of each calzone.

Pop the pan of calzones in the oven and bake 9-10 minutes or until dough is golden brown.

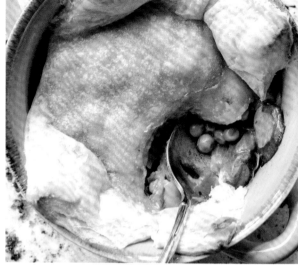

Tex-Mex Sausage Corn Chowder

Corn chowder is one of my very favorite meals. On a cold night, there is just nothing I want more than a cozy bowl of chowder... while wearing my fuzzy socks, of course! I made this Tex-Mex version with Rotel tomatoes and chili powder. Flavorful and comforting. Just what you need to warm up!

INGREDIENTS

1 pound sausage (I use an Italian pork sausage)

Extra virgin olive oil

1 onion, chopped

1½ tablespoons chili powder

Salt and pepper

2 potatoes, peeled and chopped (the smaller you chop the potatoes, the faster the soup will cook)

3 cups milk

1 (10 ounce) can Rotel tomatoes

1 (4 ounce) can chopped green chilies

1 (14 ounce) can creamed corn

1 cup fresh or frozen corn

Shredded cheddar cheese to garnish

Chopped cilantro to garnish (optional)

In a large pot over medium-high heat, brown sausage in a drizzle of olive oil. Once sausage is browned and crumbly, add in chopped onion, chili powder, and a pinch of salt and pepper. Sauté a minute or two until onions are soft.

Next, add in chopped potatoes, milk, Rotel, chopped green chilies, and creamed corn. Simmer 20 minutes (or until potatoes are tender), stirring often. Once potatoes are fork-tender, stir in fresh or frozen corn and heat through another 5 minutes.

Ladle soup into bowls and garnish with shredded cheddar and cilantro.

Beef and Ale Shepherd's Pie

When we were in London, Andrew had a shepherd's pie with beef and ale and after taking a bite, I knew we needed to recreate that. For my recipe, I made four individual servings but you could make one big serving in an 8 x 8 baking dish.

INGREDIENTS

1 pound stew meat (or a pound of flank steak chopped into bite-sized pieces)

1 cup chopped mushrooms (I use cremini)

1 onion, chopped

Salt and pepper

Extra virgin olive oil

2 tablespoons butter

2 tablespoons flour

1 cup ale

2 cups frozen or fresh peas

A few tablespoons fresh thyme, chopped

1 box of ready to bake puff pastry sheets (I use a 17 ounce Pepperidge Farm kind), at room temp

Preheat oven to 400 degrees. Lightly spray with cooking spray either one (8 x 8) baking dish or four oven safe bowls. Set aside.

In a large skillet or Dutch oven, add chopped stew meat or steak to a drizzle of olive oil over medium-high heat. Brown on all sides. Add in chopped onion and mushrooms. Do not salt and pepper until the mushrooms have completely browned up. (If you salt them before they're brown, it will take forever to get them to brown.)After everything is sautéed and tender (about 6 or 7 minutes) add a healthy pinch of salt and pepper. Add in butter and whisk in flour for about a minute. After a minute, slowly pour in ale and keep whisking. Once thickened, stir in peas and thyme. Reduce heat and simmer about five minutes.

At this time, pour the steak mixture into your baking dish(es). Fit puff pastry sheets into pan. Make sure the pastry covers the entire top.

Pop your shepherd's pie into the oven and bake about 10 minutes or until the pastry is lightly browned. Remove from the oven and serve immediately.

White Chicken Chili

Every mama needs more than one chili recipe as a go-to cozy-night meal. This one is super fast, super simple, and super delicious. It's just plain super! You pile everything in, ignore it all day, and then it's ready for you at dinnertime, yummy and hearty without any fuss. Enjoy chili night!

INGREDIENTS

1 pound boneless, skinless chicken breasts (frozen or thawed)

1 onion, chopped

1 can cream of chicken soup

1 cup tomatillo or green chili salsa

1 (4 ounce) can chopped green

chilies

1 (15 ounce) can Great Northern beans, drained and rinsed

1 cup water or chicken stock

Pepper Jack cheese and/or chopped green onions to garnish

In a slow cooker, layer chicken, onion, soup, salsa, green chilies, beans, and water (or chicken stock). Cover and cook on low for 6 to 8 hours or on high for 3 to 4 hours. Use two forks to shred the chicken right inside the slow cooker.

Ladle the chili into bowls and garnish with cheese and/or onions.

Stew

My mother-in-law's stew is so hearty and warm on a chilly evening—and even better, it's made in one pot! Even if you think you're not a "stew" person, give this a try. It converted me, and I think it could convert even the biggest stew cynic!

INGREDIENTS

1 pound stew meat, uncooked

1 tablespoon vegetable oil

4 cups water

2 tablespoons honey

1 tablespoon lemon juice

1 tablespoon Worcestershire sauce

1 onion, chopped

1 clove garlic, chopped

2 bay leaves (fresh or dried)

$1/2$ teaspoon paprika

Salt and pepper

1 cup baby carrots (or 2 large carrots, chopped)

2 potatoes, peeled and chopped

$1^1/2$ tablespoons cornstarch

$1^1/2$ tablespoons water

In a large, oven-proof Dutch oven, brown the stew meat in vegetable oil for 5 to 7 minutes. Add water, honey, lemon juice, Worcestershire sauce, onion, garlic, bay leaves, paprika, and plenty of salt and pepper. Then either cook at 275 degrees in the oven for 5 to 6 hours or cook on top of the stove for about 2 hours. In both cases, cover the Dutch oven with a lid.

If you're cooking the stew all day in the oven, about 1 hour before you're ready to eat, add the carrots and potatoes, cover, and return the stew to the oven to finish cooking. If you're cooking the stew on the stove top, then about 30 minutes before you're ready to eat, add the carrots and potatoes, cover, and finish cooking on the stove.

About 10 minutes before you're ready to serve, stir the cornstarch and water together in a little bowl until combined. If the pot is in the oven, set it back on the stovetop. Add the cornstarch mixture. Turn the heat on the stove up to medium-high and let the stew bubble away uncovered for 10 minutes, stirring occasionally. The cornstarch mixture will thicken the stew.

Ladle the stew into bowls and serve.

Mexican Meatloaf

This meal is super simple to whip up on busy weeknights, and it's the perfect mix-and-match meal. You'll love this Mexican spin on things! This recipe makes four large portions, but it can easily be doubled using a 9 x 13 baking pan for 8 servings.

INGREDIENTS

1 pound ground beef

1 cup Saltine cracker crumbs (that's about 12 crackers)

2 eggs, beaten

about 8 green onions, chopped (reserve a few for garnish)

1 (4.5 ounce) can chopped green chiles

2 tablespoons chili powder

1 (15 ounce) can black beans, rinsed and drained

2 cups of your favorite salsa, divided

1 (8 ounce) can tomato sauce

Preheat oven to 350 degrees.

Grease an 8 x 8 baking dish. Set aside.

Combine ground beef, cracker crumbs, eggs, chopped green onions, green chiles, chili powder, beans, and one cup salsa in a large mixing bowl. Pour mixture into prepared baking dish and bake 30 minutes.

Meanwhile, combine remaining cup salsa and can tomato sauce in a bowl. Once 30 minutes is up, top meatloaf with sauce and return to oven for 10 minutes.

Remove from oven and garnish with a few chopped green onions.

Pizza Meatballs

Well, this idea just makes sense. My kids love pizza and they love meatballs, so I make some meatballs that taste like pizza. Andrew and I usually eat our meatballs with a side salad, but my kiddos love theirs over buttered noodles. No matter how you serve them, they'll eat them. Simple and yummy—the perfect family combination!

INGREDIENTS

1 pound ground beef	2 eggs
1 onion, chopped	1/2 cup pepperoni, chopped
2 to 3 cloves garlic, chopped	1 (14 ounce) jar pizza sauce
2 tablespoons Italian seasoning	Parmesan cheese, grated to garnish
1/2 cup mozzarella cheese, shredded	

Preheat the oven to 425 degrees.

Line a baking sheet with foil and spray with cooking spray for easy cleanup. Set aside.

In a large mixing bowl, combine the ground beef, onion, garlic, seasoning, cheese, eggs, and pepperoni. Shape the meat mixture into 12 golf-ball-sized meatballs.

Place meatballs on the prepared baking sheet and roast them for 15 to 18 minutes or until lightly browned.

Remove from the oven and drizzle pizza sauce on top with a sprinkle of Parmesan before serving.

Chicken and Dumplings

Is any meal more comforting than chicken and dumplings? Growing up, this meal was a staple in our household and we had it every time it was cold outside. This recipe is so easy that you'll think I left something out. Trust me, I didn't! Remember, dumplings have a doughy texture. Your biscuits will be cooked, but they're not going to fluff up like biscuits.

INGREDIENTS

1 pound boneless, skinless chicken breasts, uncooked (frozen or thawed)	2 cans cream of chicken soup
	1 tablespoon black pepper
4 cups water	1 can refrigerated biscuits

Place chicken breasts in slow cooker. Top with water and both cans of soup. Add black pepper.

Cover and cook on low for 7 to 8 hours or high for 3 to 4 hours. About 15 minutes before you're ready to eat, use two forks to shred the chicken in the slow cooker.

Quarter each biscuit (I just tear them with my hands). Put biscuit pieces in slow cooker. Cover and continue to let the biscuits cook for another 15 minutes, then serve.

To make this dish on the stove top, cook the chicken over medium-high heat with 4 cups water. Then shred the chicken in the pot, add soup, and cook for about 10 minutes. Add the biscuits and cook for another 10 minutes before serving.

Spaghetti and Meat Sauce

Does any meal say "family supper" more than spaghetti and meat sauce? Spaghetti is always a hit at our house, which makes this mama really happy! You can use either ground beef or ground turkey in this recipe, so use what you love.

INGREDIENTS

1 pint cherry tomatoes

Small amount of extra virgin olive oil

Salt and pepper

1 pound spaghetti (or less if you don't want a lot of pasta)

1 pound ground beef or turkey

1 onion, chopped

3 cloves garlic, chopped

1 (28 ounce) can San Marzano tomatoes (or can whole, peeled tomatoes)

1 tablespoon Italian seasoning

Parmesan cheese and basil to garnish (optional)

Preheat the oven to 425 degrees.

Spread cherry tomatoes on a foil-lined baking sheet. Drizzle olive oil over the tops and sprinkle liberally with salt and pepper. Roast the tomatoes in the oven for about 15 minutes. (You can omit this step and just add an extra can tomatoes into the meat sauce, but I love the added flavor of roasted tomatoes.)

Over medium-high heat, bring a large pot of water to a boil and drop the spaghetti to cook until al dente (about 8 minutes).

Meanwhile, over medium-high heat, brown the ground beef or turkey in a skillet with a drizzle of olive oil and some salt and pepper. Once browned and crumbly, add the onions and garlic and sauté them for a couple of minutes. Turn heat to low and add the tomatoes and Italian seasoning. With a wooden spoon, gently break up the whole tomatoes in the skillet, then add the roasted tomatoes and gently break them up too. I like to stir a little basil and Parmesan right into my meat sauce, but you can garnish with them instead.

Drain the water from the pasta and add the pasta to the meat sauce. Serve with a sprinkle of Parmesan and a little basil (optional).

Turkey and Spinach Lazy Lasagna

This lasagna makes a great potluck or freezer meal. Bake it almost an hour if it's frozen. Also, I don't bother with boiling lasagna noodles; I just use whatever pasta I have! You can also use ground beef instead of turkey.

INGREDIENTS

2 cups pasta, any kind

1 onion, chopped

1 tablespoon extra virgin olive oil

2 pinches of salt and pepper, divided

1 pound ground turkey

3 cloves garlic, chopped

1 box frozen spinach, thawed and drained of excess water

1½ tablespoons Italian seasoning

¼ cup milk

½ cup Parmesan cheese, grated

1½ cups mozzarella cheese, grated

Preheat the oven to 350 degrees. Grease an 8 x 8 baking dish (I use cooking spray). Set aside.

Bring a pot of water to boil over medium-high heat and drop the pasta. Cook until al dente (6 or 7 minutes).

Meanwhile, in a large skillet over medium-high heat, sauté the onion in 1 tablespoon olive oil. Add a pinch of salt and pepper. After a few minutes, add the ground turkey with another pinch of salt and pepper. Cook until the turkey is browned and crumbly. Stir in garlic and spinach. Add Italian seasoning. Once spinach and garlic are combined with the turkey, slowly stir in milk and Parmesan cheese and combine.

Drain water from the pasta and layer half in the prepared baking dish. Add a layer of ground turkey mixture, followed by a second layer of pasta, and then a second layer of ground turkey. Top everything with grated mozzarella cheese.

Bake uncovered for about 20 minutes or until the mozzarella cheese is melted and everything is starting to bubble. Remove from the oven and serve.

Chicken and Ranch Pasta

This right here is the perfect busy weeknight supper. You put everything in the slow cooker that morning and then, after your long and busy day, dinner is done.

INGREDIENTS

1 pound chicken breasts

1 can cream of mushroom soup

1 (8 ounce) package cream cheese

2 cups chicken stock

1 packet dry ranch salad dressing seasoning

3 tablespoons cornstarch

3 tablespoons cold water

1 pound penne pasta cooked and drained

Parmesan cheese to garnish

Chopped green onions to garnish

Place chicken breasts across the bottom of your slow cooker. Next, pour over cream of mushroom soup, add in cream cheese. (Don't worry, it will all melt together later. Just plop it in.) Pour in chicken stock and sprinkle in ranch dressing mix. Cover and cook on low for 7 to 8 hours or on high for 3 to 4 hours.

Once you're about 15 minutes from dinnertime, boil water and drop pasta in. While the pasta is cooking, remove lid from slow cooker so some of the moisture can evaporate. Take two forks and shred the chicken right in the slow cooker. At this point, stir your cornstarch and cold water together in a separate little bowl and then stir the combined mixture into the slow cooker. This just thickens the sauce up.

Once the pasta is finished cooking, drain and then portion out on plates and top with ranch chicken mixture.

Mushroom Sausage Kale Pasta

I've used a nice chicken sausage for this pasta dish, but you can substitute turkey sausage or pork sausage. (Ask your butcher about buying good-quality chicken or turkey sausages.) If you're not into kale, feel free to substitute fresh spinach. Even with kale, though, my kiddos eat it up. Just mix and match it for your family!

INGREDIENTS

1 tablespoon extra virgin olive oil

1 pound Italian sausage (turkey, chicken, or pork)

1 pound pasta, any kind

1 shallot, chopped (or half an onion and one clove garlic)

2 cups mushrooms, chopped, any variety

4 cups kale, torn into bite-sized pieces

1 cup chicken stock

1 cup Parmesan cheese, grated

Splash of half-and-half, whipping cream, or milk

Salt and pepper

In a large skillet over medium-high heat, drizzle 1 tablespoon of olive oil. Add the sausage and begin to brown.

On a second burner, bring a large pot of water to boil. Drop the pasta and cook to al dente (about 6 to 7 minutes).

Once the sausage is browned and crumbly, add the shallot and sauté just a minute or so. Add the mushrooms and kale. Stir in the chicken stock and deglaze the pan (scrape the little bits off the bottom). Reduce heat to medium and allow the mixture to bubble up a few minutes.

Drain the pasta and add to the sausage mixture. Stir in the Parmesan cheese and a splash of half-and-half, whipping cream, or milk. Add just a pinch of salt and pepper and serve, with a bit more Parmesan to garnish if desired.

Slow Cooker Stroganoff

For this simple slow-cooker dish, I buy stew meat because it's already tender and cut into one-inch pieces. But you can use flank steak or beef tips too as long as you cut the meat into pieces. As this delightful dinner cooks in your kitchen all day, you can look forward to a big bowl of stroganoff that evening— maybe with cozy, fuzzy socks and some TV!

INGREDIENTS

1½ to 2 pounds stew meat

1 tablespoon extra virgin olive oil

Salt and pepper

1 onion, chopped

1 (14 ounce) can beef broth

1 can cream of mushroom soup

1 (8 ounce) package cream cheese, softened

2 tablespoons Worcestershire sauce

1 teaspoon garlic powder

1 pound egg noodles

Parsley to garnish, chopped

Over medium-high heat, brown the stew meat in 1 tablespoon of olive oil and some salt and pepper (about 5 minutes). Transfer the meat to the slow cooker.

Layer the onion, broth, soup, cream cheese, Worcestershire sauce, and garlic powder in the slow cooker. Cover and cook on low for 6 hours or on high for 3 hours.

About 30 minutes before you're ready to eat, move the heat to high on the slow cooker and add the noodles. Continue cooking uncovered until the noodles are tender (about 30 minutes). Sprinkle chopped parsley to garnish.

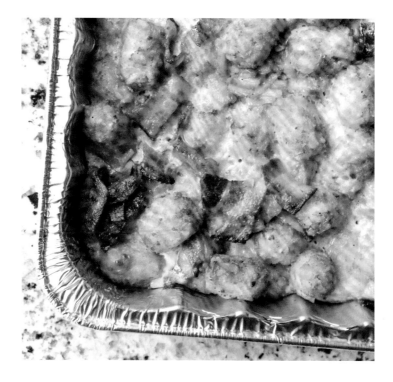

Bacon and Tot Casserole

I wanted to bring an egg-based breakfast casserole to church, and as I was reaching for hash browns at the grocery store, I saw the tater tots looking back at me and well... a better idea was born. Serve this hearty breakfast on a cool morning, and your family will gobble it up!

INGREDIENTS

1 (32 ounce) package of frozen tater tots

8 eggs

10 pieces of thick cut bacon (uncooked), chopped

8 chopped green onions

½ cup shredded Cheddar cheese

½ cup shredded Pepper Jack cheese

Salt and pepper

Preheat oven to 350 degrees. Grease a 9 x 13 baking pan. Spread your frozen tater tots across the bottom of your baking pan. Set aside.

In a mixing bowl, whisk eggs. Stir in the bacon pieces, onions, cheeses, and a big pinch of salt and pepper. Pour over the tater tots. Bake uncovered about 35 minutes or until lightly browned and bubbly. Remove from oven and serve immediately.

Oatmeal Four Ways

*Oatmeal is one of my favorite things to make and eat in the morning. It's sim-
ple, it's hot, and it's versatile. On a crazy morning, all you do is whip up one
batch of your favorite oatmeal or steel cut oats and then each of your kiddos
can top it any way they like. Let them mix and match it!*

Toasted Coconut and Macadamia Nut Oatmeal

For this topping, I just place a handful of shredded coconut and macadamia nuts
in a clean, dry skillet and toasted them for about 2 minutes together. Then, sprinkle the toasted goodness on top of your oatmeal. Simple and done!

Walnut Butterscotch Oatmeal

This topping is such a cinch! Just sprinkle a handful of butterscotch chips and
walnut pieces on top of hot oatmeal. The chips will get all melty and delicious
running through your breakfast.

Cinnamon Strawberry Oatmeal

A dash of cinnamon and a few sliced strawberries is all you need for this simple
topping and then you're out the door to start your day!

Lemon Blueberry Oatmeal

A handful full of blueberries and a little lemon zest. . .Perfection. Lemon and
blueberries were made for each other.

Butterfinger Blondies

I had been seeing different versions of Butterfinger bars float-ing around, so I decided to take my basic bar method and make it Butterfinger. Not only are these really simple, they're really yummy too!

INGREDIENTS

1 box yellow cake mix

1/2 cup vegetable oil

3 eggs

5 regular sized Butterfinger Candy Bars, chopped (about 3 cups of chopped candy)

1 stick butter, softened

3 cups powdered sugar

Splash milk

Preheat oven to 350 degrees. Grease a 9 x 13 baking dish. Set aside. In a mixing bowl, combine cake mix, vegetable oil, and eggs with an electric mixer. Stir in one cup crushed Butterfinger. Pour batter into prepared pan and bake 20 minutes or until a toothpick inserted in the middle comes out clean.

While the bars are cooling, prepare your frosting. In a mixing bowl, combine butter and powdered sugar with a splash of milk. Add more sugar if it's too thin or more milk if it's too thick. Once frosting reaches desired consistency, stir in remaining 2 cups of Butterfinger candy. Top cooled bars with Butterfinger frosting. Refrigerate bars at least 2 hours before slicing and serving.

Butterscotch Peach Cobbler

My great-grandmother's cobbler is my favorite comfort food in life. I've mixed and matched that basic recipe and turned it into a Butterscotch Peach version. Who knew that butter-scotch and peaches mingled so well together? My Mother Brooks would be proud.

INGREDIENTS

1 cup sugar

1 cup flour

1 teaspoon baking powder

1 (3.4 ounce) box of instant butter-scotch pudding mix

3/4 cup milk

4 tablespoons butter, melted

2 cups of either frozen peaches or peaches from a can (drained)

1 cup butterscotch chips

Preheat oven to 400 degrees. In a medium size mixing bowl, com-bine sugar, flour, baking powder, pudding mix, milk, and butter with a whisk. Pour into a greased 8 x 8 baking dish. Add peaches on top of the mixture in baking dish and then sprinkle butter-scotch chips on top. Bake 35 to 40 minutes or until browned and bubbly. Serve warm with ice cream for an extra something special.

Chocolate Cinnamon Bread Pudding

We love bread pudding around here. This version is full of yummy chocolate and cinnamon. It's topped with maple syrup and perfect for dessert or even breakfast. This recipe is a staple in my house, and I hope you make it a staple in your house too.

INGREDIENTS

1 loaf challah torn into pieces	1 tablespoon vanilla
4 cups milk	2 tablespoons cinnamon
3 eggs, lightly beaten	1 cup chocolate chips
1 cup sugar	Maple syrup to drizzle
1 cup brown sugar	

Preheat oven to 325 degrees (if baking that day). Place torn bread in a lightly greased 9 x 13 pan. Pour milk over bread and let it stand about 10 minutes. Using hands, blend bread and milk mixture well.

Stir eggs together with the next 4 ingredients. Stir in chocolate chips. Pour this mixture over your bread mixture. At this point, you can cover and refrigerate your casserole ovenight or you can go ahead and bake it. When you're ready to bake it, bake uncovered for 40 to 45 minutes.

Slice and serve with maple syrup on top.

You can, of course, *mix and match* it. If your grocery store bakery doesn't sell challah, you can substitute torn brioche or 8 large croissants, torn. Challah, brioche, and croissants will each give you the buttery and fluffy bread you need. If you don't want to use chocolate chips, you can either leave them out or substitute chopped pecans, dried cranberries, butterscotch chips, etc. Change it up to make your family happy.

Vanilla Bean Poppy Seed Cupcakes

I love anything vanilla bean and anything with poppy seeds! So I married the two together to make one delicious cupcake.

INGREDIENTS

$1\frac{3}{4}$ cups flour	2 eggs
$1\frac{3}{4}$ cups sugar	1 vanilla bean, split down the center
1 teaspoon baking soda	4 teaspoons poppy seeds (divided)
$\frac{1}{2}$ teaspoon salt	2 cups powdered sugar
$\frac{2}{3}$ cup butter, softened, plus another $\frac{1}{2}$ cup butter, softened	1 tablespoon milk
1 (8 ounce) container sour cream	

Preheat the oven to 350 degrees. Line 1 (12-count) muffin tin with cupcake liners and then a second muffin tin halfway full of liners (you will yield about 18 cupcakes). Set aside.

In a large mixing bowl, combine flour, sugar, baking soda, and salt with a whisk. Set aside.

In a second mixing bowl, beat with an electric mixer 2/3 cup softened butter with the sour cream and eggs. Slowly beat the flour mixture into this bowl. Once incorporated, beat in half of the seeds from vanilla bean (reserve the other half for the frosting) and 2 teaspoons of poppy seeds.

Pour batter into prepared cupcake liners (batter will be nice and thick) and bake 18 to 20 minutes or until a toothpick inserted into the center of one cupcake comes out clean.

Allow cupcakes to cool completely before frosting.

To make the frosting, beat 1/2 cup softened butter with powdered sugar and milk. Add more powdered sugar if the frosting is too thin and more milk if it's too thick. Once frosting reaches desired consistency, beat in the other half of the seeds from your vanilla bean and two teaspoons of poppy seeds. Frost cooled cupcakes.

Store in the fridge when you're not enjoying.

Boston Cream Whoopie Pies

These little whoopie pies are so cute and so simple... Plus they taste delicious! If you have a Boston Cream Pie lover in your house, you have to make these. Stat.

INGREDIENTS

1 box yellow cake mix

½ cup vegetable oil

2 eggs

¼ cup water

1 small (3 ounce) box of instant vanilla pudding mix

2 cups cold milk

Store-bought chocolate frosting

Preheat oven to 350 degrees. Combine cake mix, oil, eggs, and water in bowl. Drop by 2 tablespoons onto lined cookie sheet (leave about an inch between each cookie). Bake 8 to 9 minutes. Cool on pan 5 minutes, move to wire rack, and cool 15 more minutes.

While the cookies bake and cool, prepare your pudding. Using a wire whisk, beat your pudding mix into 2 cups of cold milk. Beat by hand for 2 minutes. Once pudding mixture thickens (after about 2 minutes), place bowl in the refrigerator to chill at least 20 minutes (about the time it takes to bake and cool your cookies).

Once your cookies are completely cooled, take one cookie and place a tablespoon or so of pudding in the center. Press another cookie on top (this will spread the pudding out to the edge). Repeat with all of your whoopie pies.

After they're all sandwiched with pudding, add a dollop of frosting to the top of each one.

Keep refrigerated until you're ready to serve.

You will have extra pudding left over. If you want to simplify this recipe even more, just use the little individual snack packs of vanilla pudding. You will probably only need about 3 to make 12 Whoopie Pies.

Mississippi Mud Bars

Chocolate base, nice marshmallow center, and yummy chocolate frosting on top...The perfect trifecta.

INGREDIENTS

1 box chocolate cake mix

1/2 cup vegetable oil

2 eggs

1 cup pecan pieces

1 (10 ounce) bag of mini marshmallows

1/2 cup butter, softened

3 cups powdered sugar

1 tablespoon milk

2 tablespoons unsweetened cocoa powder

Preheat oven to 350 degrees. Grease a 9 x 13 baking dish. Set aside. In a large mixing bowl combine cake mix, vegetable oil, and eggs with an electric mixer. Pour batter into prepared baking dish and bake 15 minutes. Remove from oven and quickly sprinkle pecans over the top, followed by the entire bag of marshmallows. Return to oven and bake another 3 minutes.

Remove from oven and allow to cool completely on the counter before frosting.

To make the frosting, beat the butter, powdered sugar, milk, and cocoa powder with an electric mixer. Add more powdered sugar if the frosting is too thin and more milk if it's too thick. Once it reaches the desired consistency, frost the cooled bars. Store in the fridge when not enjoying.

You know you're in love when you can't fall asleep because reality is finally better than your dreams.

~Dr. Seuss

FEBRUARY

DINNER

Chipotle Chicken Tostadas

Taco Joes

Spinach Pesto Baked Tacos

Spinach and Swiss
Meatballs over Quinoa

Mushroom and Beef
Crescent Casserole

Slow Cooker Balsamic Chicken

Chicken Pot Pie

Creamy Tomato and
Sausage Fettuccine

Quick Chicken Parmesan

Chicken Sausage Pasta

Sausage and Provolone Pasta

BREAKFAST

Cinnamon Roll Cups

Raspberry Lemon Rolls

DESSERT

Strawberry Nutella Pies

Peanut Butter Bars

Cherry Berry Cobbler

Tiramisu

Red Velvet M&M Brownies

Strawberry Buttermilk Cupcakes

Chipotle Chicken Tostadas

I saw little appetizers similar to this on Pinterest and decided to make a meal of them. I don't know why, but I think tostadas are way more fun to eat than a taco (even though they're basically the exact same thing!). It's like eating all our favorite taco ingredients piled up on one big crunchy chip. Genius!

INGREDIENTS

Tostada shells (right next to taco shells)

1 pound chicken breasts (thawed or frozen, it doesn't matter)

1 (10 to 15 ounce) jar of your favorite salsa

1 (7 ounce) can chipotles in adobo sauce (right there on the Mexican food aisle), divided

Guacamole

1 onion, chopped

2 tablespoons extra virgin olive oil

Salt and pepper

Cheddar cheese, sour cream, extra salsa to garnish

In a slow cooker, add in your chicken and enough water to cover. Cover and cook on low 7 to 8 hours if frozen or 4 to 5 hours if thawed.

When you're about ready to serve, remove two peppers from your can of chipotles and chop them up. In a small bowl, combine salsa with the two chopped peppers and just a teaspoon or so of the adobo sauce (in the can with the peppers). Set aside.

In a large skillet over medium-high heat, heat up olive oil a minute or two. Toss in chopped onion and a generous amount of salt and pepper and sauté until tender (about 15 minutes) stirring occasionally.

Once chicken is finished cooking, remove it to a separate bowl and shred with two forks. Discard all liquid. Toss shredded chicken in the salsa mixture.

Top tostada shell with guacamole, sautéed onion, chicken, and cheese. You can also add sour cream, extra salsa, and chopped green onion.

Taco Joes

One night I decided to make a Taco Joe, and it was spectacular! I use mild chili beans to make them more kid friendly, but you can use what your family likes. This is a meal you can throw together in minutes on a busy school night, and your family will be in love with this Joe!

INGREDIENTS

1 pound ground beef (or turkey or chicken)

1 (10 ounce) can Rotel tomatoes

1 (15 ounce) can chili beans

1 (4 ounce) can chopped green chilies

1 packet taco seasoning

3 burger buns

2 cups Cheddar cheese, shredded

Chopped green onions to garnish

Preheat the oven to 425 degrees.

In a skillet over medium-high heat, brown the ground beef until crumbly. Stir in the tomatoes, chili beans, green chilies, and taco seasoning. Reduce heat to low and simmer about 10 minutes.

On a baking sheet foil-lined for easy cleanup, lay out 6 burger bun halves. Spoon ground beef mixture on top of each half. Top each Joe with cheese.

Place the baking sheet in the oven and bake for about 10 minutes, or until the cheese looks nice and bubbly. Remove from the oven and serve with chopped green onions over the top.

Spinach Pesto Baked Tacos

You can mix and match this a million different ways. Trade out your fillings for beans, chicken, fresh spinach...go nuts! And listen...the tacos get so crispy that you'll never go back to unbaked tacos again.

INGREDIENTS

1 tablespoon extra virgin olive oil

1 pound ground beef (or ground chicken or turkey)

1 packet taco seasoning

1 box frozen spinach, thawed and drained of excess water

1 cup store-bought pesto

2 cups salsa

2 cups Monterey Jack cheese, shredded

5 taco shells (I use the "stand and stuff" ones, but regular ones will work)

Preheat oven to 425 degrees.

Heat 1 tablespoon olive oil over medium-high heat in a skillet. Add the ground beef and cook it until browned and crumbly. Stir in the taco seasoning, spinach, pesto, and salsa. Reduce the heat to low and simmer for 3 to 4 minutes.

In an 8 x 8 baking dish, line up your 5 taco shells and divide the ground beef mixture between them. Top the tacos with cheese and pop the dish into the oven. Bake for about 10 minutes or until the cheese is bubbly and brown.

Spinach and Swiss Meatballs over Quinoa

If your kiddos aren't into quinoa, put your meatballs over brown rice or pasta. You can even serve them plain alongside a green salad. Also, if your family isn't into Swiss cheese, sub with Cheddar or Monterey Jack. Mix and match it! This is a one pound meal, so you can use ground turkey or chicken in place of the ground beef if you like.

INGREDIENTS

1 pound ground beef

1 (10 ounce) box of frozen spinach, thawed and all excess water squeezed out

½ red onion, grated (just use your cheese grater or finely chop)

1 cup Swiss cheese, grated

1 cup breadcrumbs

2 eggs, lightly beaten

1 tablespoon Dijon mustard

Extra virgin olive oil

Salt and pepper

1 cup quinoa, rinsed under cold water and then drained

1½ cups chicken stock or water

Preheat oven to 425 degrees. Line a baking sheet with foil (for easy cleanup) and then lightly spray with cooking spray. Set aside.

In a mixing bowl, combine ground beef, spinach, grated onion, Swiss cheese, breadcrumbs, eggs, Dijon, and a big pinch of salt and pepper. Once combined, roll into balls and place on baking sheet. Roast 15 to 18 minutes.

Meanwhile, add your rinsed quinoa and chicken stock to a small pot over medium-high heat and bring to a boil. Once it begins to boil, cover and reduce heat to low and simmer another 15 minutes. Do not remove the lid while it's simmering. After 15 minutes, remove the lid and fluff with a fork. Drizzle in just a tiny bit of olive oil or a tablespoon of butter and a nice pinch of salt and pepper.

Serve meatballs over quinoa.

For a little more flavor in your quinoa, use chicken stock, but if you don't have any on hand, water will do just fine.

Mushroom and Beef Crescent Casserole

We could eat this casserole every week. It's hearty, it's filling, it's full of protein, and it's simple to boot. I also love this because you can easily double it to serve eight. Whether you're making dinner at home for four or you need a bigger casserole for a group, this one has your name all over it.

INGREDIENTS

1 (8 ounce) can crescent rolls

1 pound of ground beef

1 cup chopped mushrooms (I use crimini)

1 onion, chopped

1 (8 ounce) can tomato sauce

½ cup ketchup

3 tablespoons Worcestershire sauce

1 tablespoon brown sugar

½ cup grated Parmesan cheese

Extra virgin olive oil

Salt and pepper

Preheat oven to 350 degrees and grease a pie plate.

Place half of the crescent rolls across the bottom of your pie plate. Save the other half for a future use. Pop pie plate in the oven and bake rolls for 5 minutes.

Meanwhile, in a large skillet over medium-high heat, brown up your ground beef in a drizzle of olive oil. Once browned, add in mushrooms and onion and sauté about five minutes. Once mushrooms are browned up, add in a pinch of salt and pepper (don't salt until the mushrooms are browned). Next, stir in tomato sauce, ketchup, Worcestershire sauce, and sugar.

Remove pie plate from oven and pour ground beef mixture over the top. Pop pie plate back in the oven and heat through about 6 or 8 minutes.

Remove from oven and garnish with a little Parmesan cheese.

Slow Cooker Balsamic Chicken

One afternoon at our daughter's gymnastics, my friend Heather shared this simple slow cooker meal with me. She said to layer everything in my slow cooker, cover and cook all day. That's it! I love getting recipes like this one from my girlfriends!

INGREDIENTS

3 to 4 tablespoons extra virgin olive oil

1 pound boneless, skinless chicken breasts, uncooked (frozen or thawed)

1 onion, sliced

4 to 5 cloves garlic, chopped

1 (28 ounce) can fire-roasted tomatoes

½ cup balsamic vinegar

Salt and pepper

2 tablespoons sugar

In a slow cooker, layer all ingredients in the order above, omitting the sugar (you'll add that at the end). If the chicken is frozen, cook on low for 7 to 8 hours or high for 4 to 5 hours. If chicken is thawed, cook on low for 6 hours or high for 3 hours.

About 30 minutes before you're ready to eat, shred the chicken right inside the slow cooker with two forks. Stir in the sugar and cover again to finish cooking another 20 to 30 minutes before you serve.

Chicken Pot Pie

Whenever I have a really bad day...I'm talking a really, really bad one...my favorite feel-better supper is a big bowl of Chicken Pot Pie enjoyed on the couch while in my PJs and fuzzy socks. Whether you need a feel-better supper or not, this Chicken Pot Pie is sure to make you smile.

INGREDIENTS

1 tablespoon butter

1 pound cooked chicken, chopped

2 cups frozen vegetable medley

1 can cream of chicken soup

1 cup milk

Salt and pepper

1 can refrigerated biscuits

Preheat the oven to 425 degrees.

Melt butter in an oven-safe skillet over medium-high heat (you can use a baking dish later if you don't have an oven-safe skillet). Add the cooked chicken, frozen veggies, soup, and milk, with a generous amount of salt and pepper. Heat through for about 5 minutes. (Transfer this mixture into an 8 x 8 baking dish now if necessary).

Top the mixture with biscuits and pop the skillet or dish into the oven. Bake for 8 to 10 minutes or until the biscuits are brown and the chicken mixture is bubbly. Remove from the oven and serve.

Creamy Tomato and Sausage Fettuccine

Sometimes I crave a good, comforting bowl of sausage fettuc-cine—especially with cream. Because sometimes a girl needs a little creamy pasta.

INGREDIENTS

1 pound fettuccine pasta (or spaghetti)

1 tablespoon extra virgin olive oil

1 pound Italian sausage (chicken, turkey, or pork sausage)

1 shallot, chopped (or a small onion)

3 cloves garlic, chopped

1 (15 ounce) can diced tomatoes

1 tablespoon Italian seasoning

1 (8 ounce) can tomato sauce

Salt and pepper

3 tablespoons cream (half-and-half, whipping cream, or milk)

Parmesan cheese, grated to garnish

Bring a large pot of water to a boil and cook the pasta to al dente (6 to 7 minutes).

Meanwhile, over medium-high heat, brown the sausage in 1 tablespoon of olive oil. Once it's browned and crumbly, add the shallot or onion, and garlic. Sauté for a few minutes. Reduce the heat to low and stir in the diced tomatoes, Italian seasoning, and tomato sauce. Sprinkle in a little salt and pepper. Simmer for about 5 minutes. Stir in cream.

Drain the water from the cooked pasta. Stir the pasta into the tomato sauce and combine. Ladle the pasta into bowls and garnish with a little cheese.

Quick Chicken Parmesan

This is one of my hubby's favorite dinners. It's so simple, so quick to prepare...and baked! No messy frying going on here. I serve this dish with pasta and tomato sauce.

INGREDIENTS

³/₄ cup Bisquick mix

2 tablespoons Italian seasoning

2 heaping tablespoons Parmesan cheese, finely grated

1 egg, beaten

1 pound boneless, skinless chicken breasts, uncooked

2 tablespoons butter, melted

Preheat the oven to 400 degrees.

In one shallow dish (I use a pie plate), combine the Bisquick, Italian seasoning, and cheese. In a second shallow dish, beat the egg. Dip each chicken breast first in the Bisquick mix, coating well, then in the egg mix, coating both sides. Then dip them one more time in the Bisquick mix.

Place the chicken on a foil-lined cookie sheet sprayed with cooking spray. Brush half the melted butter over the tops of the chicken and bake 8 minutes. Flip the chicken over and brush the remaining half of melted butter on the opposite side and finish cooking another 8 minutes. Your chicken should be brown and kind of crispy with the juices running clear.

Chicken Sausage Pasta

I just love me a pasta dinner. For this recipe, I use chicken sausage links from the butcher counter, but you can definitely substitute pork sausage or turkey sausage.

INGREDIENTS

1 pound rigatoni pasta (I use whole wheat)

2 tablespoons extra virgin olive oil

1 pound chicken sausage links, cut into bite-sized pieces

1 red bell pepper, diced

1 onion, chopped

1 cup chicken broth

1/2 cup half-and-half

Salt and pepper

1 cup mozzarella cheese, shredded

1/2 cup Parmesan cheese, grated

Bring a large pot of water to boil, drop the pasta, and cook until al dente (7 to 8 minutes).

Meanwhile, over medium-high heat, heat 2 tablespoons of olive oil. Once hot, add sausage to brown (about 6 minutes). Let it brown and caramelize without stirring it too often. Add the bell pepper and onion, and sauté for another 5 minutes. Add the chicken stock, half-and-half, and lots of salt and pepper. Deglaze the pan (scrape the little bits off the bottom). Lower the heat to medium-low and simmer for 3 to 5 minutes. Drain the pasta and add it to the sausage mixture. Stir in the cheeses to melt, then serve.

Sausage and Provolone Pasta

This dinner is so good! I mean, seriously, you'll-have-seconds (maybe even thirds!) good. And it's super easy to put together on a weeknight. Here's the deal with the optional crushed red pepper flakes: My kids eat this pasta up, so I don't think it's too spicy. The tiny bit of heat just adds loads of flavor to the tomatoes. And the provolone cheese makes this dish rock!

INGREDIENTS

2 tablespoons extra virgin olive oil

1 pound ground sausage

1 onion, chopped

3 to 4 cloves garlic, chopped

1 pound rigatoni pasta

1/2 teaspoon crushed red pepper flakes (optional)

1 (28 ounce) can San Marzano tomatoes

1 bay leaf (fresh or dried)

1 cup chicken stock

2 to 3 tablespoons heavy cream (or half-and-half or milk)

Handful of Parmesan cheese

1/3 pound provolone cheese

Preheat the oven to 400 degrees.

In a large oven-safe skillet (or if you don't have one, transfer to a glass 8 x 8 baking dish later), heat olive oil over medium-high heat. Brown the sausage until crumbly and cooked through. Add onions and garlic and sauté for 5 to 6 minutes. Add the crushed red pepper flakes (optional), tomatoes, bay leaf, and chicken stock. Reduce the heat to medium-low and simmer for about 10 minutes, or longer if you have time.

While sauce is simmering, bring a large pot of water to a boil. Drop the pasta and cook to al dente (about 7 to 8 minutes). Drain the pasta and add the tomato mixture. Stir in the half-and-half, whipping cream, or milk, and Parmesan. At this point, if your skillet isn't oven-safe, transfer the pasta to a glass baking dish. Top the skillet or baking dish with provolone cheese. Put the casserole in the oven to brown on top and get bubbly (about 15 to 20 minutes).

Cinnamon Roll Cups

Cinnamon rolls are a big deal at our house. My kids love them, I love them...I mean, who doesn't love them? For this recipe, I flatten each biscuit inside the muffin tin and then fill it with a yummy cinnamon roll frosting mixture. Weekend mornings never tasted so good.

INGREDIENTS

¹/₄ cup granulated sugar

2¹/₂ tablespoons cinnamon, divided

1 (16 ounce) can refrigerated biscuits
(I use Pillsbury Grands)

1 (8 ounce) package of cream cheese,
softened

1 cup powdered sugar

1 tablespoon milk

1¹/₂ cups combination of your favorite
cinnamon roll toppings (walnuts, pecans,
raisins, etc.)

Preheat oven to 350 degrees.

In a small mixing bowl, combine sugar and ¹/₂ tablespoon of cinnamon with a fork. Set aside.

Take each biscuit out of the can and flatten them out just a little bit. Dredge both sides of the biscuits in your sugar mixture and then place in your lightly greased 12-count muffin tin. Push the biscuits down across the bottom and up the sides of each muffin cup. Bake about 12 minutes or until lightly browned. Remove from oven and cool just a minute or two.

While your biscuit cups are baking, beat cream cheese, powdered sugar, remaining 2 tablespoons cinnamon, and milk with an electric mixer. Once the mixture is nice and incorporated, stir in your favorite cinnamon roll toppings. (We like 1 cup of pecan pieces and ¹/₂ cup raisins.)

Once your biscuits have cooled just a minute, pop them out of the muffin tin. Take a spoon and open up the inside just a little (they will puff up, so you're opening it up). Spoon filling into each muffin cup.

Raspberry Lemon Rolls

If you're not a raspberry fan, then mix and match this any way you like... Peach, blackberry, strawberry, apple, and nutella would be delicious in this recipe too!

INGREDIENTS

1 can refrigerated crescent rolls

1 (6 ounce) container of fresh raspberries

1 lemon, the zest and juice

Preheat oven to 350 degrees. Line a baking sheet with parchment paper (for easy cleanup) and lightly spray with cooking spray.

Unroll the can crescent rolls into one rectangular sheet on your baking sheet. Press the perforations together so that your rectangle doesn't come undone. Set aside.

In a bowl, mash your raspberries with a potato masher or big spoon. Add in about half a tablespoon of lemon zest and then a tablespoon of lemon juice.

Spread raspberry mixture down the center of your rectangle. Roll the dough starting with one of the short ends to form a log. Once your dough is a log, slice it into 8 pieces and place them on the baking sheet.

Bake rolls 12 to 14 minutes. Remove from oven and serve immediately.

Strawberry Nutella Pies

*I'm always looking for a little dessert to make just for two peo-
ple. Some nights, you just want to stay home with your sweetie
and indulge without baking an entire cake or pan of brownies.
This would be perfect for a Valentine's dinner at home. I made
mine with Nutella and strawberry pie filling, but you can totally
mix and match this up. Here are some other ways you could
make your pies...*

INGREDIENTS

Fudge Sauce and Cherry
Pie Filling

Apple Pie Filling

Peach Pie Filling

Nutella

Pumpkin Pie Filling

Caramel Sauce with Apple Pie Filling

Nutella with Raspberry Jam

Fudge with Orange Marmalade

Sprinkle in chopped pecans,
walnuts, dried cranberries, coconut,
chocolate chips, butterscotch chips...

Here's how you assemble them. Unroll defrosted pie crusts. (I use
2 sheets of pie crust to make 4 pies. You could just use one sheet
and then only have 2 pies. You need a bottom piece and a topper
piece for each pie.) Use a large cookie cutter or a bowl to get 4
pieces of dough.

Lay your bottom pieces out on a baking sheet. Spread a little
Nutella across the middle of each one. Next, add a dollop of pie
filling. Then take your topper pieces and top the bottom pieces.
I pinch the edges down so that everything stays inside the pie.
Sprinkle the tops of the pies with a little sugar.

Bake at 350 degrees for about 10 minutes.

Peanut Butter Bars

*Peanut butter reigns supreme at our house and every time I
start to make a bar, my two oldest go, "Can it be peanut butter?" Bless them. One day I said, "Sure..." and thus a new family
favorite was born.*

INGREDIENTS

1 box yellow cake mix

4 eggs

1 stick melted butter

1 box powdered sugar
(about 4 cups)

1 (8 ounce) package cream
cheese, softened

1 cup creamy peanut butter

Preheat oven to 350 degrees. Grease 9 x 13 pan and set aside.

In a mixing bowl, combine cake mix, 2 eggs, and melted butter.
Spread in bottom of pan to form crust layer.

In a second bowl, beat the powdered sugar, 2 remaining eggs,
cream cheese, and peanut butter until smooth with an electric
mixer. Spread cream cheese mixture on top of crust mixture. Bake
35 to 40 minutes until edges are brown and center set (it will still
be slightly wobbly in the middle).

Cool on counter 30 minutes, then refrigerate 2 hours or up to 2
days. Slice into bars and serve.

Cherry Berry Cobbler

I just cannot stop making this cobbler. We just love, love, love it! It's simple to make and delicious every time. I also think this would make a yummy Valentine's Day dessert. After a special meal, you could enjoy this delicious cobbler with the one you love.

INGREDIENTS

1 (10 ounce) package of frozen mixed berries (do not thaw)

1 (21 ounce) can cherry pie filling

1 yellow cake mix

1 stick butter, melted

Ice cream, optional

Preheat oven to 350 degrees. Grease a 9 x 13 baking dish.

Spread frozen berries across the bottom of baking dish. Next, spoon pie filling on top of the frozen berries and then sprinkle the box of dry cake mix on top of the fruit. Finally, drizzle the melted butter over everything.

Bake uncovered 55 to 60 minutes. Remove from oven and serve immediately (with a little ice cream if you so desire).

Tiramisu

Tiramisu is a great make-ahead dessert for any occasion. I made this one 24 hours before we enjoyed it. Tiramisu always looks fancy but is really simple.

INGREDIENTS

6 egg yolks

1¼ cups sugar

1¼ cups mascarpone cheese

1¾ cups heavy whipping cream

1 (12 ounce) package ladyfinger cookies

⅓ cup coffee flavored liqueur or brewed coffee brought to room temp

Semi-sweet chocolate chips to sprinkle on top

Before you begin, place a glass or ceramic mixing bowl in the freezer along with a pair of beaters so that they get nice and cold.

Fill a small saucepan halfway full of water and place over medium-high heat. Bring to a gentle boil and then place a glass bowl on top (to create a double boiler). Combine egg yolks and sugar in the glass bowl and whisk constantly until it reaches a boil over double boiler. Reduce heat to low and continue to whisk another minute or two. When it starts to thicken up, remove from heat and whisk the mascarpone cheese into the yolk mixture. Whisk until combined. Discard water in saucepan.

Remove mixing bowl and beaters from the freezer. Pour in whipping cream and beat with an electric mixer until stiff peaks form. Once they form, gently fold the yolk mixture into the whipped cream with a rubber spatula. Set aside.

Line the bottom of serving dish with ladyfingers (you're going to make layers, so just line it with first layer). Lightly brush the ladyfingers with either coffee liqueur or brewed coffee. Spoon half of the cream filling over the ladyfingers and repeat with another row of cookies, followed by more coffee and more filling. End with a final row of ladyfingers on top. Sprinkle chocolate chips on top.

Cover and refrigerate at least 4 hours or up to 24 hours.

Red Velvet M&M Brownies

You'll swoon over the simplicity and deliciousness of these brownies! They're the perfect Valentine's Day treat.

INGREDIENTS

1 box red velvet cake mix

2 eggs

⅓ cup vegetable oil

1 cup M&Ms (I use Valentine's Day ones), plus a few extra for garnish

Preheat oven to 350 degrees. Grease a 9 x 13 baking dish. Set aside.

Combine the first 3 ingredients in a mixing bowl with a spoon (batter will be thick). Stir in M&Ms.

Spread batter across the bottom of prepared pan and bake about 14 minutes or until a toothpick inserted in the middle comes out clean.

After you pull the warm brownies out of the oven, sprinkle a few extra M&Ms on top. Cut into squares and serve.

Strawberry Buttermilk Cupcakes

The key is the buttermilk...it makes everything more dense and moist. I even kept a dozen of these beauties unfrosted and served them as "muffins" the next morning. Perfection.

INGREDIENTS

For the cupcakes:

$\frac{1}{2}$ cup butter, softened

1$\frac{1}{2}$ cups sugar

2 eggs

1 teaspoon vanilla

1$\frac{1}{2}$ cups flour

1 teaspoon baking soda

$\frac{1}{2}$ teaspoon salt

1 cup buttermilk

1 cup chopped strawberries

For the frosting:

$\frac{1}{2}$ cup butter, softened

3 cups powdered sugar

A splash or two of buttermilk

1 teaspoon vanilla

1 cup chopped strawberries

Preheat oven to 350 degrees. Line 2 (12 count) muffin tins with paper liners.

In a large mixing bowl, cream butter and sugar together. Next, beat in one egg at a time. Beat in vanilla. In a second large bowl, combine flour, baking soda, and salt together with a spoon. Slowly beat a little of the flour mixture into butter mixture. Then beat in a little buttermilk. Repeat two or three times or until everything is incorporated. Do not overbeat your batter. Stir in strawberries.

Fill each cupcake liner $2/3$ of the way full of batter. Bake 15 to 20 minutes or until a toothpick inserted in the middle comes out clean.

Let cupcakes rest in pan 10 minutes before moving them to a wire rack to finish cooling.

To make frosting, beat your butter with powdered sugar. Add in a splash of buttermilk. Add more buttermilk if your frosting is too thick and more powdered sugar if it's too thin. Once it reaches the desired consistency, stir in vanilla and chopped strawberries.

Frost cooled cupcakes. Keep any leftovers refrigerated.

If you're lucky enough to be Irish,
you're lucky enough.

~Irish Saying

MARCH

DINNER

Spinach, Sausage, and Feta Pizza

Spinach Calzones

Jolly Green Joes

Spinach and Sausage
Stuffed Potatoes

Taco Stuffed Peppers

Sour Cream and Chicken
Enchilada Stack

Green Onion and Spinach Turkey
Meatballs

Pizza Enchiladas

Fiesta Chicken with Rice

Sausage and Kale Risotto

BREAKFAST

Sausage and Cheese Muffins

St. Patrick's Day Pancakes

DESSERT

Key Lime Bread

Key Lime Pie Bars

Irish Cream Pie

Grasshopper Pie

Lucky Shamrock Mix

Creamy Mint Brownies

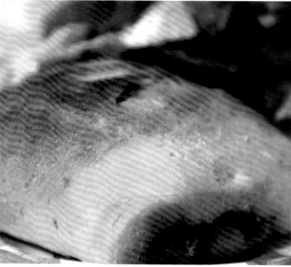

Spinach, Sausage, and Feta Pizza

We love little pizzas with a biscuit crust. These are easy to assemble (your kiddos can help!) and great for simple suppers. Just add a salad and dinner is done!

INGREDIENTS

1 (16 ounce) can refrigerated biscuits (I use Pillsbury Grands)

2 tablespoons Italian seasoning blend

1 pound Italian sausage

1 (10 ounce) jar of pizza sauce

about 2 cups fresh spinach

1 red onion, chopped

1 cup feta cheese

extra virgin olive oil

Salt and pepper

Preheat your oven to 400 degrees. Line a cookie sheet with foil and grease with cooking spray for easy cleanup.

Open can of biscuits and press out each one onto your prepared cookie sheet. I just press mine out to make them a little more flat than they come out of the can. Put just a drizzle of olive oil on the tops of each biscuit and then sprinkle Italian seasoning over each one. Pop your biscuits in the oven and toast about five minutes.

Meanwhile, in a large skillet over medium-high heat, brown Italian sausage. Remove to a paper towel. Next, add chopped red onion right inside your skillet with the sausage drippings. Add in a pinch of salt and pepper.

Pull biscuits out of the oven and spread a little pizza sauce over the top of each one. Next, lay a few pieces of spinach down followed by a scoop of your sausage. Sprinkle your sautéed red onions over the top. Return the cookie sheet back to the oven and bake your little pizzas another five minutes. Remove from oven and sprinkle feta over the tops of each pizza. Serve immediately.

Spinach Calzones

You can buy the ingredients for this versatile recipe way in advance and keep them in your fridge for last-minute meals. These calzones take no time to prepare, and you can mix and match a million ways. If your family doesn't love spinach, leave it out. If you prefer browned sausage, go for it! If you would rather throw in a ton of chopped veggies with no meat, be my guest!

INGREDIENTS

Drizzles of extra virgin olive oil

1 box frozen spinach, thawed and drained of excess water

3 cloves garlic, chopped

1 can refrigerated pizza dough (or any pizza dough you love and have on hand)

1 (10 ounce) jar pizza sauce

Turkey pepperoni (or whatever meat you like)

1 cup mozzarella or Italian blend cheese

Preheat the oven to 425 degrees.

Line a baking sheet with foil and spray with cooking spray for easy clean up.

In a small skillet, heat a drizzle of olive oil over medium heat. Add the spinach and stir for 2 to 3 minutes. Add the garlic and cook for another minute. Remove from heat.(You're just getting the spinach warm and infused with the garlic.)

Spread the dough into a rectangle and cut into four squares. On one half of each square, put 2 tablespoons pizza sauce. Then layer 5 to 6 pepperoni, 2 tablespoons or so of the spinach mixture, and a few tablespoons of cheese. Fold the other half of the square on top. Press the sides down to seal in all the filling. Cut two little slits across the top of each calzone with a knife. Then brush each with a drizzle of oil. Bake for 9 to 10 minutes or until the dough is golden brown.

Jolly Green Joes

The Jolly Green Joe was born when I was trying to think of a sloppy joe I could serve on St. Patrick's Day. Ground turkey plus spinach, green bell pepper, green chilies, green onions, avocado—all jolly and green and perfect for a St. Paddy's Day supper (or any old night for that matter!).

INGREDIENTS

1 pound ground turkey

Drizzle of extra virgin olive oil

Pinch of salt and pepper

1 (10 ounce) package frozen spinach, thawed and drained of excess water

1 green bell pepper, chopped

1 (4 ounce) can chopped green chilies

1½ cups green chili or tomatillo salsa

8 to 10 green onions, chopped

Burger buns

1 avocado, pit removed and sliced into pieces

In a large skillet over medium-high heat, brown the turkey in a drizzle of olive oil until browned and crumbly. Add a liberal pinch of salt and pepper. Stir in the spinach, bell pepper, green chilies, salsa, and onions (saving a few to garnish). Reduce the heat to medium and let the mixture simmer for about 5 minutes or until everything is heated through.

Top each burger bun with a generous portion of ground turkey mixture. Garnish with pieces of avocado and a few remaining chopped green onions.

Spinach and Sausage Stuffed Potatoes

This dish is super filling, so the next time you need a simple supper, just stuff it! For this recipe, use one box of frozen spinach for four baked potatoes, adjusting how much spinach you use according to the size of your family. You can also "twice bake" these potatoes in the oven, fully loaded. Then bake for 5 minutes at 350 degrees.

INGREDIENTS

1 (10 ounce) box frozen spinach, microwaved

4 large russet potatoes

1 (8 ounce) container sour cream

1 cup Monterey Jack cheese, shredded

1 big handful chives, snipped into little pieces

Salt and pepper

4 fully cooked turkey sausage links, chopped into bite-sized pieces

Microwave spinach until heated through. It will be hot! I cooked mine for 5 minutes and then used a clean kitchen towel to squeeze out all the water over the kitchen sink.

I like to bake my potatoes at 300 degrees for about an hour, but you can microwave them. Once potato is fully cooked, slice each one open and "fluff" up the inside with a fork.

Add 1/4 cooked spinach to each potato. Stir in 1/4 of the sour cream, cheese, and chives, along with a generous pinch of salt and pepper. Add the sliced sausage and serve.

Taco Stuffed Peppers

I just love me a taco, a stuffed pepper, and an easy dinner. So here you go: a stuffed bell pepper that tastes like a taco and is on the table in no time. This makes me happy inside. By the time these tacos are finished cooking, the peppers are so nice and soft and easy to eat with just a fork. Remember, two peppers equal 4 servings.

INGREDIENTS

2 large bell peppers, any color

Drizzle of extra virgin olive oil

1 pound ground beef (or chicken or turkey)

1 packet taco seasoning (or two heaping tablespoons of chili powder)

Salt and pepper

1 cup salsa

1 can chopped green chilies

1/2 cup frozen corn

1 cup cooked rice (I use brown)

2 cups Cheddar cheese

Preheat the oven to 425 degrees.

Slice each bell pepper in half, length-wise. Remove the stem and seeds. Place pepper halves in an 8 x 8 baking dish. Drizzle olive oil over the tops of the peppers and bake about 10 minutes.

While the peppers are baking, brown the ground beef over medium-high heat on the stove. Once brown and crumbly, sprinkle in the taco seasoning and a bit of salt and pepper. Stir in the salsa, chilies, corn, and rice, and reduce the heat to low.

Remove the peppers from the oven and stuff with the ground beef mixture (keep peppers in baking dish). Sprinkle the cheese over all 4 peppers, then pop them back into the oven and cook for another 15 minutes.

Remove from the oven and serve.

Sour Cream and Chicken Enchilada Stack

I love to make Enchilada Stacks because they're like layered casseroles that taste just like an enchilada. Lots of flavor, little work. That's the best kind of weeknight meal!

INGREDIENTS

1 pound cooked chicken breast, shredded

1 box chopped frozen spinach, thawed and drained of excess water

2 tablespoons butter

2 tablespoons flour

1 cup half-and-half

1 cup milk

1 (4 ounce) can chopped green chilies

4 green onions, chopped

3 cloves garlic, chopped

1 tablespoon cumin

½ teaspoon crushed red pepper flakes

2 cups Monterey Jack cheese

6 to 8 tortillas (I use whole wheat)

Sour cream to garnish

Preheat the oven to 400 degrees.

Melt the butter in a saucepan over medium heat. As soon as the butter is melted, whisk in the flour. Whisk for about a minute and then whisk in the half-and-half and milk. Bring the mixture to a bubble, then cook and stir for about 2 minutes or until the mixture has thickened quite a bit. Stir in the spinach, chilies, onions, garlic, cumin, and red pepper flakes. Remove from heat.

In an 8 x 8 casserole dish, spread ⅓ of the spinach mixture across the bottom. Layer in half of the chicken, sprinkle in ⅓ of the cheese, and top with a layer of tortillas. Repeat. Finish with the remaining ⅓ spinach mixture and ⅓ cheese on the top. Cover with foil and bake for 20 to 25 minutes. Remove the foil and bake for another 5 minutes. Garnish with sour cream and serve.

Green Onion and Spinach Turkey Meatballs

This is what happens when you let your four-year-old help you plan dinner—you get a theme like green and off you go! Kensington loves meatballs and said she wanted green ones. Hmm, easy enough. Not only were they yummy but they were packed full of veggies too. Score for Mom! Let's all be thankful Kensington didn't want pink meatballs!

INGREDIENTS

1 pound ground turkey (or beef or chicken)

1 box frozen spinach, thawed and drained of excess water

10 green onions, chopped

1 egg

1 cup panko or breadcrumbs

½ cup Parmesan cheese, grated

Pinch of both salt and pepper

2 tablespoons extra virgin olive oil

1 (8 ounce) jar pesto

Preheat oven to 400 degrees.

In a large bowl, combine the first 8 ingredients (turkey through olive oil). Shape the mixture into golf-ball-sized meatballs and place them on a baking sheet lined with foil and sprayed with cooking spray to make cleanup easy. With a tablespoon or so, top each meatball with some pesto.

Bake for about 25 minutes or until the juices run clear and the meatballs are brown and cooked through.

Pizza Enchiladas

Pizza. Enchiladas. I mean...Life's short, right? Why not? Your kids are going to love these!

INGREDIENTS

1 pound ground Italian sausage (I use pork but you could use chicken)

2 cups pepperoni, sliced thin or chopped

1 (14 ounce) bottle pizza sauce

1/2 cup grated Parmesan cheese

1 cup chopped basil, plus a little more to garnish

8 flour tortillas

1 (8 ounce) can tomato sauce

1 1/2 cups shredded mozzarella cheese

Extra virgin olive oil

Preheat oven to 375 degrees. Grease an 8 x 8 inch baking dish. Set aside.

In a large skillet over medium-high heat, brown sausage until crumbly in a drizzle of olive oil. Once browned, lower the heat to medium and stir in pepperoni, pizza sauce, and Parmesan cheese along with chopped basil. Heat through a few minutes.

Next, take each flour tortilla and spoon a little of the pizza filling down the center and then roll up. Place inside your prepared baking dish. Repeat until all eight tortillas are rolled and tightly placed inside dish. Next, pour tomato sauce over the enchiladas and then sprinkle the mozzarella cheese on top.

Pop the enchiladas into the oven and bake about 30 minutes, or until cheese is browned and everything is bubbly.

Remove from oven and serve immediately with a little extra basil to garnish.

Fiesta Chicken with Rice

This Fiesta Chicken with Rice is easy, easy and yummy, yummy! Dinner with minimal ingredients and maximum flavor? That's a weeknight miracle, and I'm a happy mama!

INGREDIENTS

1 pound boneless, skinless chicken (frozen or thawed)

2 tablespoons chili powder

1 can cream of chicken soup

2 cups salsa

2 cups cooked rice (I use brown rice)

Cheese and chopped green onions to garnish

Place the chicken in a slow cooker. Sprinkle the chili powder over the chicken and then top with the soup and salsa. Cook on low for 6 to 8 hours (8 if the chicken is frozen) or on high for 3 to 4 hours (4 if the chicken is frozen).

Shred the chicken right inside the slow cooker with two forks. To serve, layer cooked rice and chicken on each plate, then top with cheese and/or green onions.

Sausage and Kale Risotto

Risotto intimidates people, even though it's so simple! It takes less than 30 minutes to prepare. The large container or bag of Arborio rice you typically have to buy will also last in your pantry for a long time. Use precooked turkey, pork, or chicken sausage, or even leftover chicken, plus whatever veggies you have on hand.

INGREDIENTS

2 quarts chicken stock

2 tablespoons extra virgin olive oil

1 pound precooked sausage links, cut into pieces

1 small onion, chopped

2 cloves garlic, chopped

1 cup Arborio rice

2 cups fresh kale, torn into pieces

1/2 cup sundried tomatoes, removed from the oil in the jar and lightly chopped

1/2 cup Parmesan cheese, grated

Salt and pepper

In a large pot, bring the chicken stock to a low simmer (not boiling, just a simmer). Keep a lid on it to trap liquid inside.

In a separate pan, heat 2 tablespoons of olive oil over medium-high heat, add the sausage, and sauté for 4 to 5 minutes to get it a little brown. Once it's brown, remove it with a slotted spoon to a paper towel and reserve.

Add the onion and garlic to the skillet and cook for 4 to 5 minutes. Stir in the rice for another minute.

At this point, ladle 1 cup of the hot chicken stock into the rice. Stir constantly for a minute or so. As the liquid evaporates, the rice will become super starchy and delicious. Stir pretty often, adding stock every time the majority of the liquid evaporates. You will continue doing this for about 18 minutes. Add stock, stir, wait for it to evaporate, and add more. This will cause the risotto to fluff up and look creamy (without using any cream!). A lot of recipes tell you to stir continuously, but you don't need to. Just stir every few minutes and you'll be fine.

Once the rice is tender (take a bite!), stir in the fresh kale and sundried tomatoes and continue cooking for another 3 to 4 minutes. Stir in the cheese and reserved sausage. Season with salt and pepper to taste.

Sausage and Cheese Muffins

These make the perfect quick breakfast, lunchbox treat, or after school snack. You can even freeze them and then pop them in the microwave for 30 seconds to warm up. This recipe makes about 20 muffins.

INGREDIENTS

1 pound breakfast sausage, uncooked

4 cups Bisquick

2½ cups milk

2 eggs

1½ cups shredded Cheddar cheese

Preheat oven to 400 degrees. Line 2 (12-count) muffin tins with muffin liners. Set aside.

In one mixing bowl, crumble in your uncooked breakfast sausage. Next, stir in your dry Bisquick mix. Using a wooden spoon, mix the two together. (They're not going to totally combine. Don't overwork it.)

In a second bowl, whisk together your milk and eggs. Slowly pour this mixture over your sausage mixture. Stir together until everything is combined. Next, stir in your cheese.

Divide batter (it will be lumpy!) among your muffin tins. I was able to get 20 muffins out of this batter.

Place muffins in oven and bake about 20 minutes or until lightly browned. Remove from oven and serve immediately or store.

St. Patrick's Day Pancakes

Who needs Green Eggs and Ham when you can have Green Pancakes instead? Since I know how much my kiddos love my cake batter pancakes, I decided to make a batch and turn them green for St. Patrick's Day. Such a big hit! In fact, my kiddos loved it so much that they requested Green Pancakes the following day too.

INGREDIENTS

1 box white cake mix

½ cup flour

2 eggs

2 cups milk

½ cup vegetable oil

A few drops of food coloring

Preheat griddle to medium-high. Combine all ingredients in a large mixing bowl with a whisk.

Ladle pancake batter onto greased griddle and let sit until you see bubbles rise up. Once they get bubbly, flip them over and cook the other side. It only takes about 4 minutes to cook them total.

Keep ladling and flipping pancakes until the batter is gone. This recipe yields about 18 pancakes.

Key Lime Bread

I just love making quick breads. They come together in minutes, they slice and serve beautifully and they work for breakfast, dessert, and snack time. Because it's a little green, this would be a fun bread to make and share with others around St. Patrick's Day.

INGREDIENTS

For the bread:

2 eggs

1 cup sugar

³/₄ cup vegetable oil

Juice and zest of 2 key limes (about 2 tablespoons of juice and 1 tablespoon of zest)

1¹/₄ cup flour

¹/₂ teaspoon baking soda

¹/₂ teaspoon salt

For the glaze:

1 key lime (juice and zest)

1 cup powdered sugar

Preheat oven to 350 degrees. Lightly spray one loaf pan with cooking spray. Set aside.

In a large mixing bowl, beat eggs until light and frothy. Beat in sugar and oil. Stir in key lime juice and zest. Set aside.

In a second mixing bowl, combine flour, baking soda, and salt and mix together with a fork.

Slowly beat flour mixture into key lime mixture. Beat until just combined.

Pour batter into prepared pan and bake 40 to 45 minutes. A toothpick inserted in the center of the loaf should come out clean when the bread is done.

Allow the bread to cool at least 20 minutes before removing it from the pan to finish cooling.

To make the glaze, combine powdered sugar with the juice of one key lime and its zest. Add more powdered sugar if it's too thin or more zest if it's too thick. Drizzle glaze over bread when you're ready to slice and serve.

Key Lime Pie Bars

This dessert makes me think spring is in the air. The flavor combination is a marriage made in bar heaven. If you can't find key limes at your grocery store, you can use a regular lime instead. You'll need 4 key limes or 2 regular limes for this recipe.

INGREDIENTS

1 box of yellow cake mix

4 eggs

¹/₂ cup butter, melted

1 box powdered sugar (about 4 cups)

8 ounce package cream cheese, softened

2 tablespoons of key lime zest

¹/₂ cup fresh key lime juice

Preheat oven to 350 degrees. Grease a 9 x 13 baking dish.

In a large mixing bowl, combine cake mix, 2 eggs, and melted butter. Spread in bottom of pan.

In a second bowl, beat with electric mixer powdered sugar, 2 more eggs, cream cheese, lime zest, and lime juice until smooth. Spread cream cheese mixture on top of crust mixture.

Bake 35 to 40 minutes until edges are brown and center set (it will still be slightly wobbly in the middle).

Cool on counter 30 minutes, then refrigerate 2 hours or up to 2 days.

Irish Cream Pie

I was taking dinner to some friends and wanted to include a little dessert. So I took out a box of pudding, some mini graham cracker crusts, and my good old Irish Cream coffee creamer and whipped these up. For this recipe, you can use one 9-inch graham cracker crust or 6 mini ones.

INGREDIENTS

1 (3 ounce) box instant vanilla pudding

1 (14 ounce) can sweetened condensed milk

½ cup Irish Cream flavored coffee creamer

Graham cracker crusts

Whipped cream for garnish, optional

In a large mixing bowl, whisk together the pudding, sweetened condensed milk and Irish Cream for about two minutes. Pour mixture into pie crusts and refrigerate at least two hours before serving.

Garnish with whipped cream right before serving.

Grasshopper Pie

I'm always looking for a little green to make around St. Patrick's Day. And since mint chocolate is one of my very favorite flavor combinations, I use it a lot. Creamy, cool, a little minty and in an Oreo crust...I bet even the Irish would like this pie. This recipe makes two 9-inch pies. You can cut the recipe in half to only make one.

INGREDIENTS

2 pre-made Oreo pie crusts (found on the baking aisle by the graham cracker crusts)

1 (8 ounce) container Cool Whip, from the fridge not frozen

1 (8 ounce) package cream cheese, softened

1 (½ gallon) container mint chocolate ice cream, softened just a bit

In a large mixing bowl, combine the Cool Whip and cream cheese with an electric mixer. Do not over mix, just combine. Add your ice cream to the mixture and combine with a spoon (not the electric mixer). Once incorporated, divide the mixture between your two pie shells.

Cover and freeze at least 2 hours before slicing and serving.

Lucky Shamrock Mix

This is a great snack to munch on while watching movies on a chilly afternoon—and it's great to stick in kids' lunchboxes too!

INGREDIENTS

1 bag of popped popcorn (about 4 cups total)

4 cups Lucky Charms cereal

8 ounce white candy coating or almond bark

2 cups white chocolate chips

1 cup mint chocolate chips (optional)

2 cups mini marshmallows

Green sprinkles

Lay wax paper down over kitchen counters. In a large mixing bowl, combine popcorn and Lucky Charms together. In a microwavable bowl, melt candy coating, stirring every 45 seconds. Once it's melted, quickly pour it over popcorn mixture and toss.

Working quickly, add in white chocolate chips, mint chocolate chips, marshmallows and sprinkles and then pour the mixture onto the wax paper to dry (about 10 minutes). Once it's dried, store in an airtight container.

Creamy Mint Brownies

I made these and took them to church on a Sunday morning. By the time I got home at noon, I already had one text and one email from girlfriends wanting the recipe. This right here is my favorite flavor combination. Chocolate and mint are just meant to be together.

INGREDIENTS

1 box chocolate cake mix

½ cup vegetable oil

2 eggs

1 cup mint chocolate chips

1 (8 ounce) package cream cheese, softened

2 cups powdered sugar

1 splash milk

1 teaspoon peppermint extract

2 or 3 drops green food coloring

Preheat oven to 350 degrees. Grease a 9 x 13 baking dish. Set aside.

In a large mixing bowl, combine cake mix, vegetable oil, and eggs with an electric mixer until creamy. Stir in mint chocolate chips. Pour batter into prepared baking dish and bake about 10 minutes or until a toothpick inserted into the middle comes out mostly clean (do not over bake).

Remove from oven and cool completely before frosting.

To make the frosting, beat cream cheese, powdered sugar, and milk with an electric mixer. Add more powdered sugar if it's too thin or more milk if it's too thick. Once it reaches desired consistency, beat in the peppermint extract and green food coloring.

Frost cooled bars and store in the fridge when you're not enjoying.

Sweet April showers do
bring May flowers.

~Thomas Tusser

APRIL

DINNER

Crispy Chicken
with Poblano Sauce

King Ranch Joes

Pizza Quesadillas

Mom's Meatloaf

Mexican Meatballs

Bacon and Broccoli Quinoa

Spring Vegetable Risotto

Chicken and Bacon Carbonara

Spinach Pesto Pasta Bake

Pasta with Bacon and Corn

BREAKFAST

Tex-Mex Breakfast Casserole

Carrot and Zucchini Waffles

DESSERT

Plum Berry Galette

Marshmallow Peep Bars

Cadbury Crème Egg Brownies

Carrot Cake Bars

Peep Corn

Crispy Chicken with Poblano Sauce

Andrew often orders grilled chicken with a poblano sauce at one of our regular restaurants, so I decided it was time to whip up something similar. I bake Crispy Chicken instead (because our kids love it), but you can pour this sauce over any meat, poultry, or fish. Your kiddos should be able to enjoy this sauce as well; it's not too spicy with the seeds removed from the pepper.

INGREDIENTS

2 eggs

2 cups breadcrumbs

Pinch of salt and pepper

4 chicken breast halves, uncooked

1 poblano pepper, seeded and chopped into chunks

8 green onions, chopped

1 cup chicken stock

1 cup Pepper Jack or Monterey Jack cheese, shredded

Preheat the oven to 400 degrees. Line a baking sheet with foil and lightly spray with cooking spray for easy cleanup.

In one shallow dish, lightly beat both eggs (I use a pie plate). In a second shallow dish, add the breadcrumbs and a generous pinch of salt and pepper.

Dip a piece of chicken first in breadcrumbs, then in beaten egg, and then back in breadcrumbs. Place on the baking sheet and repeat with the rest of the chicken. Bake chicken for about 20 minutes or until nice and crispy and the juices run clear when pierced with a fork.

To make the poblano sauce: Place the pepper, onions (save some to garnish), and chicken stock in either a food processor or blender and pulse until blended (I leave it just a little chunky for texture). Pour the mixture into a small saucepan and bring it to a simmer over medium-high heat. Once it's nice and a little bubbly, stir in the cheese and heat until just melted.

Remove the chicken from the oven and pour poblano sauce over the top. Garnish with a few extra green onions.

King Ranch Joes

I really can't think of many things I love more than a King Ranch Casserole. Southern girls all have their favorite version of this classic, so I thought I'd make one too. If you already have shredded chicken on hand, you can skip right to the last part and let your chicken mixture just heat up in the slow cooker.

INGREDIENTS

1 pound chicken breasts

8 cups of water

1 (10 ounce) can cream of mushroom soup

1 (10 ounce) can cream of chicken soup

1 (10 ounce) can Rotel tomatoes

2 tablespoons chili powder

4 thick slices cornbread for serving

Shredded cheddar cheese to garnish

Chopped green onions to garnish

In your slow cooker, add in your chicken and water. Cover and cook on low 6 to 8 hours or on high 3 to 4 hours. About an hour before you're ready to eat, remove chicken and discard liquid. Add chicken back to hot slow cooker and shred with two forks. Next, stir in cream soups, Rotel, and chili powder. Cover and cook on high another 30 minutes to an hour.

When you're ready to serve, take each plate and place a nice thick piece of cornbread in the center. Next, add a big dollop of your chicken mixture on top. Garnish with a little shredded cheddar and some chopped green onions.

Pizza Quesadillas

Our family likes to fill these quesadillas with ground beef, pepperoni, mozzarella, and basil, but you can put whatever you love inside (ground turkey, salami, ham, bell peppers, onions, spinach...go crazy!). Next time you're looking for a simple Sunday night supper, just mix and match the quesadilla.

INGREDIENTS

1 pound ground beef

1 (14 ounce) jar pizza sauce

1 (8 ounce) jar tomato sauce

6 burrito-sized flour tortillas

1 cup or so sliced pepperoni

1½ cups mozzarella cheese, shredded

Big handful of fresh basil, torn

In a large skillet over medium-high heat, brown the ground beef until cooked through and crumbly. Stir in the pizza sauce and tomato sauce. Heat through for about 3 or 4 minutes.

Preheat the indoor griddle or a second big skillet to medium-high heat. Spray lightly with cooking spray.

Lay out 6 flour tortillas and spread ground beef across the bottom half of each one. Add sliced pepperoni, shredded cheese, and basil to each one. Fold the top part down to cover the bottom portion.

Place each quesadilla in the skillet one at a time. Brown on both sides (each side about 4 minutes). Remove once each is browned and slice it in half to make 2 quesadillas. Repeat with other tortillas.

Mom's Meatloaf

Meatloaf is my husband's favorite meal. Period. I started making my mom's recipe for him when we were dating, and if I ever ask him what he wants for dinner, this is it. It can be prepared in advance and popped into the oven at the last minute. Served with a side of mashed potatoes, this is a real man's dinner.

INGREDIENTS

1 pound ground beef

1 cup saltine cracker crumbs (about 12 crackers)

2 eggs, beaten

1 onion, chopped

1 teaspoon salt

5 tablespoons Worcestershire sauce, divided

1 (8 ounce) can tomato sauce

1 cup ketchup

²/₃ cup brown sugar

1 teaspoon mustard

Preheat the oven to 350 degrees.

Mix the ground beef, cracker crumbs, eggs, onion, salt, 3 tablespoons Worcestershire sauce, and tomato sauce in a bowl. Put the mixture in a greased 8 x 8 baking dish and bake for 40 minutes.

Meanwhile, combine the remaining 2 tablespoons of Worcester-shire sauce and the ketchup, brown sugar, and mustard in a bowl. Once the 40 minutes baking time is up, top the casserole with sauce and return it to the oven for 15 minutes.

Mexican Meatballs

Even in April, my family sometimes needs comforting, cozy food. These little Mexican meatballs are flavorful without being too spicy, super simple to prepare, and quick-cooking. This is an excellent weeknight dinner, but works well for entertaining too.

INGREDIENTS

1 pound ground beef (or ground chicken or turkey)

½ onion, chopped

3 cloves garlic, chopped

1 cup panko or breadcrumbs

½ cup Cheddar cheese, grated

1 (4 ounce) can chopped green chilies

1 packet taco seasoning (or 2 tablespoons chili powder)

2 eggs, beaten

2 splashes milk

1 to 2 tablespoons extra virgin olive oil

2 cups prepared rice (I use brown)

Salsa

Preheat the oven to 425 degrees.

In a medium bowl, combine the ground beef, onion, garlic, panko or breadcrumbs, cheese, green chilies, taco seasoning, eggs, and milk. Roll the mixture into balls (I make mine golf-ball sized) and place on a lightly greased baking pan lined with foil for easy cleanup. Drizzle 1 to 2 tablespoons of olive oil over all the meatballs. Roast them in the oven for about 20 minutes or until they are brown.

Serve over prepared rice with salsa spooned on top.

Bacon and Broccoli Quinoa

This is like a big bowl of comfort food but healthy at the same time. You can serve this as a very hearty side or as a main dish.

INGREDIENTS

2 cups quinoa

3 cups water

8 pieces bacon
(I use turkey bacon), chopped

1 shallot, chopped

Extra virgin olive oil

Salt and pepper

3 tablespoons flour

2 cups milk

1½ cups cheddar cheese, shredded

2 cups broccoli florets

½ cup grated Parmesan cheese

Before you begin, rinse your quinoa off under cold running water. Add quinoa and water to a pot over medium-high heat on the stove. Cover and bring to a boil. Once boiling, reduce heat to low and continue to simmer covered about 10 to 15 minutes.

While your quinoa simmers, place your bacon pieces in a drizzle of olive oil in a skillet over medium-high heat. Allow bacon pieces to crisp up. After they're crispy, add in your chopped shallot and a pinch of salt and pepper. Sauté the shallot a minute or two. Next, sprinkle in your flour and whisk a minute. Next, whisk in your milk and continue to whisk until sauce begins to thicken up. Once sauce starts to thicken up, whisk in your cheese and continue whisking until incorporated.

Pour cooked quinoa into skillet with bacon cheese sauce. Stir in the quinoa and broccoli florets. Sprinkle in Parmesan cheese.

Remove from heat and serve immediately with extra Parmesan.

Spring Vegetable Risotto

Risottos help you transition well into spring letting you mix and match the ingredients with fresh, seasonal veggies. You get something completely different and appropriate for the warmer days of spring: fresh, light...and simple!

INGREDIENTS

2 quarts chicken stock (use vegetable stock for a vegetarian dish)

1 tablespoon butter

Extra virgin olive oil

2 zucchini, chopped

10 pieces asparagus, chopped

1 onion, chopped

3 to 6 cloves garlic, chopped

1 cup Arborio rice

1 cup frozen peas

2 cups cooked chicken, chopped (optional)

½ cup Parmesan cheese, grated

Salt and pepper

In a large stock pot, bring the chicken stock up to a low simmer (not boiling, just a simmer, and keep a lid on it to trap liquid inside).

In a separate pan, melt the butter with 1 tablespoon of olive oil over medium-high heat. Add the zucchini and asparagus and sauté for 4 to 5 minutes. Remove the veggies from the pan, cover them, and set them aside.

Add the onion and garlic to the skillet and cook for 4 to 5 minutes. Stir in the rice for another minute.

At this point, ladle 1 cup of the hot chicken stock into the rice. Stir constantly for a minute or so. As the liquid evaporates, the rice will become super starchy and delicious. Stir pretty often, adding stock every time the majority of the liquid evaporates. You will continue doing this for about 18 minutes. Add stock, stir, wait for it to evaporate, and add more. This will cause the risotto to fluff up and look creamy (without using any cream!). A lot of recipes tell you to stir continuously, but you don't need to. Just stir it around every few minutes and you'll be fine.

Once the rice is tender (take a bite!), stir in the frozen peas, zucchini, asparagus, and chicken, and continue cooking for another 3 to 4 minutes. Stir in cheese and season with salt and pepper to taste.

Chicken and Bacon Carbonara

This is my spin on a traditional Carbonara but with a little shredded chicken thrown in for good measure. My kiddos eat this pasta up! It's not too rich, and not too heavy, but full of flavor.

INGREDIENTS

1 pound cooked and shredded chicken

1 pound spaghetti noodles

A few tablespoons extra virgin olive oil

8 slices bacon (I use turkey bacon but use what ya got!), chopped

4 cloves garlic, chopped

8 to 10 green onions, chopped

1 cup chicken stock

2 egg yolks, beaten

Handful of Parmesan cheese

Bring a large pot of water to boil and drop your pasta in to cook to al dente (about 7 to 8 minutes).

Meanwhile, in another skillet, sauté bacon in a few tablespoons of olive oil. Once bacon crisps up, add in garlic and half the green onions and sauté about a minute. Stir in chicken stock and deglaze your pan to get all the bits off the bottom. Add cooked and shredded chicken breasts to skillet. Reduce heat to medium-low and simmer.

Drain pasta but reserve about a cup of the hot cooking water. Add pasta to skillet. Pour a little bit of the hot water into the dish where you have your beaten eggs and whisk with a fork. (This will temper your eggs so they don't scramble in your skillet.) Turn skillet off and add tempered eggs to the pasta. Add the cheese and toss until the eggs and cheese are incorporated with the pasta. Top with extra cheese and a few more green onions.

Spinach Pesto Pasta Bake

For this meal, I wanted something cheesy, pesto-y, and with ground beef. Typically, pesto dishes are made with fish or chicken, but I wanted one with ground beef...so I made one. And it's really good too!

INGREDIENTS

1 pound pasta, any kind

1 pound ground beef

Several tablespoons extra virgin olive oil

1 shallot, chopped

3 to 4 cloves garlic, chopped

1 box frozen spinach, thawed and drained of excess water

1 (about 7 ounces) jar pesto

1 (3 ounce) package cream cheese, softened

Salt and pepper

1/2 cup reserved cooking liquid (after pasta cooks, reserve about 1/2 cup water from the pot)

1 cup mozzarella cheese, shredded

Parmesan cheese to garnish, grated

Preheat the oven to 425 degrees.

Bring a large pot of water to a boil and drop in the pasta. Cook to al dente (7 or 8 minutes).

Meanwhile, heat a few tablespoons of olive oil over medium-high heat in a large skillet. Add the ground beef and cook until browned and crumbly. Add the shallot and garlic and sauté for 3 to 4 more minutes. Add the spinach, pesto, and cream cheese, and incorporate into the ground beef mixture. Add salt and pepper (as much or as little as you like, probably a few good pinches).

At this time, remove about 1/2 cup water from the pasta pot. Stir the water into the pesto-groun d beef mixture. Drain the pasta and add it to the ground beef mixture as well. Pour everything into an 8 x 8 baking dish (unless you have an oven-safe skillet), top with mozzarella cheese, and bake it until it's brown and bubbly (about 15 minutes).

Remove from the oven and garnish with Parmesan.

Pasta with Bacon and Corn

Fresh corn is so good when it's in season, but frozen corn works here too.

INGREDIENTS

1 pound pasta, any kind

Several tablespoons extra virgin olive oil

10 pieces bacon (I use turkey bacon, but use whatever you like)

1 small onion, chopped

Salt and pepper

2 cloves garlic, chopped

1 cup corn kernels (fresh or frozen)

1 cup creamed style corn

$\frac{1}{2}$ cup Parmesan cheese, grated

In a large pot, bring water to a boil. Drop in the pasta and cook to al dente (about 6 to 7 minutes).

Meanwhile, in a big skillet, heat a few tablespoons of olive oil over medium-high heat. Add the bacon and cook it until crisp. Remove the bacon from the pan and reserve it on a paper towel. Add the onion and some salt and pepper and sauté for about 5 minutes. Stir in the garlic and fresh or frozen corn and cook over medium heat for another 4 to 5 minutes. Stir in the creamed corn and reserved bacon, chopped.

Drain the pasta from the pot and toss it with the corn mixture. Add the Parmesan cheese and stir until all the pasta is incorporated with the sauce. Add a little more salt and pepper to taste.

Tex-Mex Breakfast Casserole

I'm always trying to come up with new breakfast casserole recipes to serve on special mornings. Sometimes, we like to enjoy breakfast casseroles for dinner too. A slice of this with a big green salad and we're happy at supper time! Whether you're having this with coffee and juice in the morning or at dinner, your family will enjoy it.

INGREDIENTS

1 pound breakfast sausage

About 3 cups of tortilla chips, lightly broken

6 eggs, beaten

2 cups milk

1 can cream of mushroom soup

2 (4 ounce) cans chopped green chilies

1 tablespoon chili powder

2 cups cheddar cheese, divided

Brown sausage over medium-high heat until cooked through and crumbled. Meanwhile, combine eggs, milk, soup, green chilies, chili powder, and one cup cheese in a bowl.

In a 9 x 13 pan, layer cooked sausage across bottom, then layer broken-up chips. Next, pour egg mixture over. Finally, top with remaining one cup cheese. You can either cover and refrigerate overnight or bake immediately.

The next morning (or right then), bake casserole uncovered in a 350 degree oven for one hour.

Carrot and Zucchini Waffles

We love waffles. In honor of Easter, we added grated carrot and zucchini to our batter and made them a little seasonal. Plus, when you eat veggies in your waffles, they count as health food, right? I'm going to tell myself that as I enjoy seconds. This recipe will yield enough batter for four big Belgian waffles or 8 smaller waffles.

INGREDIENTS

2 cups flour

2 teaspoon baking powder

pinch of salt

2 tablespoons sugar

1 cup milk

1 egg, lightly beaten

$\frac{1}{2}$ cup grated carrot

$\frac{1}{2}$ cup grated zucchini

1 tablespoon cinnamon

Preheat waffle iron. Lightly spray with cooking spray. In a large mixing bowl, combine the flour, baking powder, salt and sugar with a whisk. In a second large mixing bowl, combine the milk and egg. Slowly whisk the wet ingredients into the dry ingredients. Combine but do not over mix. Once all combined, stir in grated veggies and cinnamon.

Ladle batter into hot waffle iron and bake to your liking. Remove and serve with your favorite maple syrup.

Plum Berry Galette

Sometimes, you just need a quick dessert. People stop by, people stay later than expected...or it's just a random Thursday night and you want something sweet. When you're thinking easy (and delish!), think galette. A galette is just a freeform pie. You take your crust, you add in whatever you like, bake, and enjoy. This is the perfect mix and match recipe.

INGREDIENTS

1 uncooked pie crust (I use a store-bought one but you can use homemade)

1 cup frozen mixed berries

2 cups sliced fresh plums (about 2-3 plums)

1½ tablespoons flour

2 tablespoons sugar (divided)

Preheat oven to 425 degrees.

Roll out pie crust onto a lightly greased baking sheet. Set aside.

In a mixing bowl, toss berries and plums with flour and one tablespoon of sugar. Spoon this fruit mixture into the center of pie crust. Fold up the edges around the crust. Take remaining tablespoon of sugar and sprinkle it over the top.

Pop the galette in the oven and bake 10 to 12 minutes. Remove from oven and serve immediately (maybe with some ice cream too!).

Marshmallow Peep Bars

I made s'mores bars but used Easter Marshmallow Peeps inside, and let me tell you, they are just so good! If you don't make anything else this Easter season, make these. In fact, go ahead and pick up a few extra packages of Peeps, because after Easter, you're still going to want to make them.

INGREDIENTS

1 box yellow cake mix

1/2 cup vegetable oil

2 eggs

16 to 20 Marshmallow Peeps (any color, just not flavored)

1/2 cup butter, softened

3 cups powdered sugar

1 tablespoon or so of milk

2 tablespoons unsweetened cocoa powder

Preheat oven to 350 degrees. Grease a 9 x 13 baking dish. Set aside.

In a large mixing bowl combine cake mix, vegetable oil, and eggs with an electric mixer. Pour batter into prepared baking dish and bake 10 minutes. Remove from oven and quickly place the Peeps in 3 rows across the pan. Return to oven and bake another 4 minutes.

Remove from oven and slightly press Peeps down just a little with the back of a spatula. Allow to cool completely on the counter before frosting.

To make the frosting, beat the butter, powdered sugar, milk, and cocoa powder with an electric mixer. Add more powdered sugar if the frosting is too thin and more milk if it's too thick. Once it reaches the desired consistency, frost the cooled bars. Store in the fridge when not enjoying.

Cadbury Crème Egg Brownies

Easter isn't complete until we make these little bars. Get your kids to help you unwrap the little eggs!

INGREDIENTS

1 box of your favorite brownie mix

2 eggs

1/2 cup vegetable oil

1/4 cup water

3 dozen miniature Cadbury Crème Eggs

Preheat oven to 350 degrees. Grease a 9 x 13 baking dish. Set aside.

In a large mixing bowl, beat with an electric mixer brownie mix, eggs, vegetable oil, and water until smooth. Pour brownie batter into prepared pan.

Unwrap miniature Crème Eggs and carefully lay them down inside the batter in rows.

Bake about 18 minutes or until a toothpick inserted in the middle comes out clean. Allow bars to cool at least 30 minutes before slicing and serving.

Carrot Cake Bars

It's not Easter if we're not eating carrot cake. Carrot cake with a nice cream cheese frosting is a staple at our Easter lunch every single year. So needless to say, a carrot cake bar was in order.

INGREDIENTS

1 box carrot cake mix

4 eggs

½ cup butter, melted

1 box powdered sugar (about 4 cups)

1 (8 ounce) package cream cheese, softened

Preheat oven to 350 degrees.

Grease a 9 x 13 baking dish.

In a large mixing bowl, combine cake mix, 2 eggs, and melted butter. Spread in bottom of pan.

In a second bowl, beat with electric mixer powdered sugar, 2 more eggs, and cream cheese until smooth. Spread on top of crust mixture.

Bake 35 to 40 minutes until edges are brown and center set (it will still be slightly wobbly in the middle).

Cool on counter 30 minutes, then refrigerate 2 hours or up to 2 days. If you can't find a box of carrot cake mix (which is usually easy to find), then substitute with a box of spice cake mix and then grate a cup of carrots into the mix before beginning.

Peep Corn

My kids and I have the best time making our Easter Peep Corn! A little popcorn, a little white chocolate, some sprinkles, and some Peeps.

INGREDIENTS

1 bag of popped popcorn (plain, not buttered or flavored)

6 ounces of white chocolate candy coating

Your favorite Easter candies (I use M&Ms, Jelly Beans, and Peeps)

Easter sprinkles

Pour popped popcorn out on a wax paper lined baking sheet.

Microwave white chocolate candy coating in a bowl, stopping to stir every 30 seconds until melted (it should only take about a minute or so).

Drizzle white chocolate over the popcorn.

Sprinkle favorite Easter candies and sprinkles over the popcorn.

Allow everything to sit at least 15 minutes before packaging up and storing in an airtight container.

Land of the free, and the home of the brave.

~FRANCIS SCOTT KEY

MAY

DINNER

Mango Chicken Tostadas

Tomatillo and Spinach Enchiladas

Candied Jalapeño Grilled
Cheese Sandwiches

Caesar Salad Burgers

Buffalo Turkey Burgers

Hawaiian BBQ Chicken Burritos

Chipotle Corn Chicken

Crispy Chicken with Mushroom
and Shallot Sauce

Lemon Poppy Seed Baked Chicken

Sausage and Leek Pasta

Shrimp Risotto

Spinach and Sundried Tomato Meatballs

BREAKFAST

Ham and Cheese
Biscuit Sliders

Lemon Monkey Bread

DESSERT

Mini Coconut Cream Pies

Hawaiian Shortcakes

Strawberry Banana Pie

Lemon Whoopie Pies

Pink Lemonade Bars

Mango Chicken Tostadas

To change up Tostada Tuesday at our house, we add a bunch of veggies and some nice mango instead of using our normal Tex-Mex flavors. By the way, frozen mangoes in a bag are divine if fresh mangoes are not available. And the coconut lovers in our house added toasted coconut. (Put your coconut in a dry skillet and brown up just slightly over medium-low heat.)

INGREDIENTS

1 pound boneless, skinless chicken breasts, uncooked

4 cups pineapple juice (plus a little water to cover)

2 cups mango chunks (fresh or frozen)

1 red bell pepper, chopped and seeded

1 avocado, chopped into chunks

8 green onions, chopped

Salt and pepper

Tostada shells

Toasted coconut to garnish (optional)

In a slow cooker, layer the chicken and add the pineapple juice. (If you still need to cover the chicken with more liquid, add water until the chicken is covered.) Cover and cook on low for 6 to 8 hours or on high for 3 hours. The last 30 minutes your supper is cooking, shred the chicken right inside the slow cooker with two forks, turn the heat to high, and add the mango and chopped bell pepper. Cover and cook the remaining 30 minutes.

Using a slotted spoon, remove the chicken, mango, and pepper and put it all into a bowl (discard the liquid). Add bits of avocado and chopped green onion. Sprinkle with salt and pepper. Top each tostada shell with the chicken mixture. If you're using toasted coconut, sprinkle it on top now.

Tomatillo and Spinach Enchiladas

Tomatillos pair perfectly with spinach to turn a basic chicken enchilada into something really special. This includes the homemade version of this salsa, but if you want to go the simple, simple route, you can buy a jar of store-bought tomatillo salsa. Either way, you're going to love the flavor combination!

INGREDIENTS

8 to 10 tomatillos, husks removed and rinsed off

3 to 4 garlic cloves

1 onion, sliced

1 jalapeño pepper, sliced (remove seeds for a less spicy version)

Juice of one lime

1 pound cooked and shredded chicken (see my perfect chicken method)

1 box frozen spinach, thawed and all of the excess water squeezed out

1 can cream of chicken soup

8 green onions, chopped

2 teaspoons chili powder

Salt and pepper

2 cups Monterey Jack cheese, shredded

8 tortillas (either flour or whole wheat)

Preheat oven to 400 degrees. Lightly spray an 8 x 8 baking dish with cooking spray. Set aside.

To make the salsa, in the bowl of your food processor, combine tomatillos, garlic, onion, jalapeño, and lime juice and pulse until salsa consistency. Set aside.

In a large mixing bowl, combine the shredded chicken with the spinach, cream of chicken soup, green onions, chili powder, a pinch of salt and pepper, and one cup Monterey Jack cheese. Add in one cup of salsa.

Once combined, take each tortilla and spread a little bit down the center. Roll and place in the prepared baking dish. Once all 8 enchiladas are tucked inside the baking dish, pour second cup of salsa over the top of them. Sprinkle enchiladas with remaining one cup shredded cheese.

Bake uncovered about 20 minutes or until the edges of the tortillas are lightly brown and everything is bubbling. Remove from oven and serve immediately with just a few more green onions for garnish.

Candied Jalapeño Grilled Cheese Sandwiches

I was finding candied jalapeño in everything at restaurants, so I decided to use them at home too. They're a sweetened yet still hot jalapeño pepper available in jars at the grocery store. They still have a nice kick, but they're mild enough that you can pop one into your mouth and eat it plain.

INGREDIENTS

2 pieces bread (I like a crunchy French loaf)

2 to 3 slices sharp Cheddar cheese

2 pieces bacon, cooked to crisp (or make vegetarian)

6 to 8 candied jalapeños

Preheat grill pan or a large skillet to medium-high. Lightly spray with cooking spray.

Assemble one sandwich (bread, cheese, bacon, jalapeños, and top with bread) then grill it until the cheese is nice and melted (flipping it over halfway). If you really want the sandwich to be decadent, add a little butter to the outside of both pieces of bread before grilling.

Once cheese is melted, slice and serve.

Caesar Salad Burgers

It's a turkey burger that tastes like a chicken Caesar salad. You pile your Caesar salad toppings on top and put everything on a big piece of Texas Toast like a giant crouton.

INGREDIENTS

2 pounds ground turkey

3 tablespoons extra virgin olive oil

2 anchovy fillets, chopped (optional)

1 cup grated Parmesan cheese, plus a little more for garnishing

1 box frozen spinach, defrosted and all of the excess liquid squeezed out

Romaine lettuce leaves torn for topping

Drizzles of your favorite Caesar Salad dressing

4 pieces Texas Toast, toasted

Preheat your outdoor grill or indoor grill pan to medium-high heat.

Add the olive oil, chopped anchovy fillets (optional), one cup Parmesan and spinach to your ground turkey. Divide turkey into four sections and make four patties. Grill patties about 8 minutes per side or until cooked through.

Add your cooked burger patty to a piece of Texas Toast and then top with Romaine lettuce and drizzles of your favorite Caesar dressing. Garnish with a little more Parmesan.

Buffalo Turkey Burgers

In my opinion, turkey burgers need to be a little fancy or else they're a lot of boring. Any time we're grilling up some turkey burgers, we try and add lots of flavor to our finished product. So, a buffalo style burger with buffalo sauce, bleu cheese, ranch dressing, and shredded carrots sounded like the best way to jazz up a basic burger. And bonus...it's ready and on your table in no time!

INGREDIENTS

2 pounds ground turkey

3 tablespoons extra virgin olive oil

Salt and pepper

½ cup of your favorite buffalo sauce (you can use more for drizzling if you like!)

1 cup shredded carrots

1 red onion, chopped

1 cup of bleu cheese crumbles

Drizzles of your favorite ranch dressing

Burger buns

Preheat your outdoor grill or indoor grill pan to medium-high heat.

Add the olive oil, salt, pepper, and buffalo sauce to your ground turkey. Divide turkey into four sections and make four patties. Grill patties about 8 minutes per side or until cooked through.

Add your cooked burger patty to your burger bun and then top with shredded carrots, chopped red onion, bleu cheese crumbles, and a drizzle of ranch dressing. Garnish with a little more buffalo sauce if you like.

Hawaiian BBQ Chicken Burritos

I'm really into sweet and spicy flavors for spring and summer, and this little twist on a burrito matches the sweetness of pineapple with the spiciness of jalapeño. Don't worry if you're serving your kiddos. This recipe is totally kid friendly, and you can just use a little less jalapeño.

INGREDIENTS

1 pound cooked chicken, shredded

1 cup BBQ sauce

1 jalapeño, seeds removed and chopped (use less if you want less heat)

1 (8 ounce) can crushed pineapple

8 to 10 green onions, chopped

5 burrito-sized tortillas

Preheat the oven to 375 degrees.

In a mixing bowl, combine the chicken, BBQ sauce, jalapeño, pineapple, and green onions.

Spoon the chicken mixture down the center of each tortilla. Roll the tortillas burrito-style (ends folded down and then folded over left and right).

Place burritos seam side down on a foil-lined baking sheet that has been lightly sprayed with cooking spray for easy cleanup. Bake for 15 to 18 minutes or until lightly browned.

Drizzle a little extra pineapple, BBQ sauce, and/or green onions over each burrito before you serve.

Chipotle Corn Chicken

This recipe is a mix-and-match spin on Fiesta Chicken with Rice. It's spicy from the chipotles and sweet from the corn, but the best part is that it's so quick and easy to make. Chipotles, sold in small cans, are spicy, so if your family is not a fan of spice, just add one. You can freeze the rest for later use. They're really good chopped up in almost any Tex-Mex dish.

INGREDIENTS

1 pound boneless, skinless chicken (frozen or thawed)

2 tablespoons chili powder

2 cups salsa

1 to 4 chipotles, chopped

1 can creamed corn

1 cup frozen corn

2 cups cooked rice (I use brown)

Cheese and chopped green onions to garnish

Place the chicken in a slow cooker. Sprinkle the chili powder over the chicken and then top with the salsa, chipotles, and creamed corn. Cook on low for 6 to 8 hours (8 if the chicken is frozen) or on high for 3 to 4 hours (4 if the chicken is frozen).

About 20 minutes before you're ready to eat, shred the chicken right inside the slow cooker with two forks. Stir in the frozen corn. Keep the lid off until you're ready to eat. This thickens the chicken mixture.

Layer the cooked rice and chicken on a plate, then top with cheese and/or green onions.

Crispy Chicken with Mushroom and Shallot Sauce

I love making crispy chicken because my kids think it's "kid food." Andrew and I love our chicken smothered with this yummy sauce but two of my kids prefer it with just some ketchup.

INGREDIENTS

4 boneless chicken breast halves

2 eggs, lightly beaten

2 cups breadcrumbs or Panko

Salt and pepper

2 shallots, chopped

2 cups coarsely chopped mushrooms (we use portobellos)

Extra virgin olive oil

2 tablespoons flour

1½ cups of white wine (we used Pinot Grigio)

Parsley to garnish

Preheat oven to 400 degrees.

Line a baking sheet with foil and lightly spray with cooking spray (for easy clean up).

In one shallow dish, lightly beat your two eggs (I use a pie plate). In a second shallow dish, add in your bread crumbs and a generous pinch of salt and pepper.

Dip each piece of chicken first in bread crumbs, then in the beaten egg, and then back in your breadcrumbs. Place on baking sheet and repeat. Bake chicken about 20 minutes or until nice and crispy and the juices run clear when pierced with a fork.

Meanwhile, in a large skillet over medium-high heat, add in several drizzles of olive oil along with your shallots and mushrooms. Sauté 5 to 7 minutes or until everything is nice and caramelized. Once the mushrooms have browned, add in a generous pinch of salt and pepper. Next, stir in your flour and whisk it around about a minute before whisking in your wine. Reduce heat to low and allow sauce to simmer about 10 minutes.

Remove the chicken from the oven and ladle the mushroom and shallot sauce over the top. Garnish with a little parsley.

Lemon Poppy Seed Baked Chicken

This meal is so simple, so delicious, and so colorful that you should serve it at least once a week in the summer. The lemon juice is all you need to dress your spinach, and the strawberry garnish is a perfect complement. If you really want to mix and match, you can grill the chicken or use another kind of salad dressing.

INGREDIENTS

4 boneless, skinless chicken breast halves

1 (16 ounce) bottle poppy seed salad dressing

4 cups fresh spinach leaves

2 lemons, sliced

Chopped red onion, sliced strawberries, and parsley to garnish (optional)

Preheat oven to 350 degrees. Lay the chicken breasts on a baking sheet lined with foil for easy cleanup. Pour $1/2$ cup salad dressing over the top of each one. Bake for about 25 minutes or until the juices run clear when pricked with a fork.

   Place 1 cup spinach on each plate. Remove the chicken from the oven and place one pieece on top of the spinach. Squeeze fresh lemon juice over the tops. If desired, garnish with chopped red onions, sliced strawberries, and a little parsley.

Sausage and Leek Pasta

I consider leeks to be onion's little sister. They're mild and versatile, especially in pasta. Here's the deal, though: Leeks are grown in sandy soil so you have to wash the outsides and the insides. The easiest way is to chop them, place them in a colander in your sink, and then run lots of cold water over them. Use a paper towel to lightly pat them dry.

INGREDIENTS

1 pound pasta (I use whole wheat rotini)

2 tablespoons extra virgin olive oil

1 pound bulk Italian sausage, either hot or sweet (or chicken sausage or turkey sausage)

3 leeks, washed and chopped

3 cloves garlic, chopped

1½ cups chicken broth

Salt and pepper

1 (6 ounce) jar sundried tomatoes in oil, drained

½ cup Parmesan cheese, grated

8 to 10 basil leaves, torn or chopped

Bring a large pot of water to boil, drop the pasta, and cook until al dente (6 to 7 minutes).

Meanwhile, over medium-high heat, heat 2 tablespoons of olive oil. Once hot, add the sausage to brown (about 6 minutes). Let it brown and caramelize without stirring it too often. Add the leeks and garlic and sauté for another 5 minutes. Add the chicken broth and lots of salt and pepper, and deglaze the pan (scrape the little bits off the bottom), lower the heat to medium-low, and simmer for 3 to 5 minutes. Stir in the sundried tomatoes.

Drain the pasta and add it to the sausage mixture. Stir in cheese and basil.

Shrimp Risotto

This meal should take you about 30 minutes from start to finish. Relax...risotto is a cinch!

INGREDIENTS

2 quarts chicken stock

2 shallots, chopped (or one red onion)

Either 8 sweet peppers chopped or 2 bell peppers

1 cup Arborio rice

1 pound peeled and deveined shrimp

1½ cups frozen or fresh corn kernels

1 pint of cherry tomatoes

½ cup Parmesan cheese, grated

Basil leaves, torn, to garnish

Extra virgin olive oil and salt and pepper, of course!

In a large stock pot, bring the chicken stock up to low simmer (not boiling, just a simmer...keep a lid on it to trap liquid inside).

In a separate pan, heat a couple of tablespoons of olive oil over medium-high heat and add in your shallots and chopped peppers and cook 4 to 5 minutes. Stir in rice for another minute.

At this point, take a ladle and add 1 cup of your hot stock to the rice. Stir constantly for a minute or so. As the liquid evaporates, the rice will become super starchy and delicious. Stir pretty often, adding stock every time the majority of the liquid evaporates. You will continue doing this for about 18 minutes. Add stock, stir, wait for it to evaporate, and add more. This will cause the risotto to fluff up and look creamy (without using any cream!). A lot of recipes will tell you to stir continuously, but you don't need to. Just stir it around every few minutes and you'll be fine.

After the rice is tender (take a bite!), stir in your shrimp, corn, and cherry tomatoes. Continue cooking another 5 to 6 minutes (it doesn't take long for the shrimp to cook up in the risotto). Stir in cheese and basil and season with salt and pepper to taste.

Spinach and Sundried Tomato Meatballs

These meatballs are like little Greek delights—feta cheese, tomatoes, spinach...delish! Usually a meatball would be a fall and winter food in our house, but these are light with ground turkey, and a little bit of lemon zest brightens them up for eating in warmer weather.

INGREDIENTS

1 pound ground turkey (or chicken)

4 cloves garlic, grated

1 cup panko or breadcrumbs

½ cup feta cheese, crumbled

1 package frozen spinach, thawed and drained of excess water

1 (6 ounce) jar sundried tomatoes

in oil, drained

2 eggs, beaten

2 teaspoons lemon zest

Salt and pepper

1 tablespoon extra virgin olive oil

Preheat the oven to 425 degrees.

In a medium bowl, combine the ground turkey, garlic, panko or breadcrumbs, feta, spinach, tomatoes, eggs, zest, and lots of salt and pepper. Form meat mixture into golf-ball-sized balls and then place them on a lightly greased baking pan lined with foil for easy cleanup. Drizzle a tablespoon of olive oil over all the balls. Roast in the oven for about 25 minutes or until brown.

Serve alone or over your favorite pesto pasta.

Ham and Cheese Biscuit Sliders

My friends love these because they're super yummy and I love them because they're so simple. It's a win-win situation. These little sandwiches are great for lunch, light suppers with a salad, as a snack, as breakfast, or as an appetizer.

INGREDIENTS

1 (16 ounce) can biscuits (I use Grands)

½ pound of deli sliced ham

½ pound thinly sliced Swiss cheese

Honey to drizzle

Preheat oven and bake biscuits per package directions.

Remove biscuits from oven and allow to cool a minute or two. Keep oven on and baking sheet out.

Slice each biscuit in half and lay the two pieces out. Top one half of each biscuit with a few pieces of ham and a few pieces of cheese. Add the top back on the biscuit and place all 8 of your sandwiches back on a foil lined baking sheet.

Drizzle a tablespoon or so of honey over each sandwich. Place baking sheet full of sandwiches back in the hot oven and bake another 5 minutes. Remove from oven and serve immediately.

Lemon Monkey Bread

Monkey breads are my favorite weekend breakfasts to make. This lemon version is my take on a summer breakfast.

INGREDIENTS

½ cup sugar

2 (16.3 ounce) cans refrigerated flaky layer biscuit dough, cut into quarters

½ cup butter

¼ cup light corn syrup

1 small box (3.4 ounce) instant lemon pudding mix, dry and not prepared

1 cup powdered sugar

1 tablespoon milk

Preheat oven to 350 degrees. Spray a Bundt pan with cooking spray. Add sugar to a small bowl. Dredge biscuit quarters in sugar to coat. Layer in prepared pan.

(At this point, you could cover your pan and pop it in the fridge until the next morning.)

In a small saucepan, combine butter, corn syrup, and instant pudding mix. Cook over medium-high heat stirring constantly until mixture comes to a boil. Boil one minute. Pour over layered biscuits. Bake 40 minutes. Let pan sit 5 minutes before inverting it onto platter to serve.

In a small bowl, whisk together powdered sugar and milk to make a glaze. Add more milk if the glaze is too thick and more sugar if it's too thin. Drizzle glaze over warm monkey bread and serve.

Mini Coconut Cream Pies

I make these little pies by using sugar cookie dough as the crust. It's such a delicious little pie, and it's super easy to mix and match. Try making a chocolate cream pie version, or pumpkin pie, or banana cream pie, or snickerdoodle pie...just to name a few!

INGREDIENTS

1 (16 ounce) tube of refrigerated sugar cookie dough (or make your own from scratch)

1 (3 ounce) box of instant coconut pudding mix

2 cups milk

2 cups sweetened coconut flakes

Preheat oven to 350 degrees. Grease two 12-count muffin tins. Slice a piece of cookie dough off of the tube and press it inside of each muffin tin to form a crust. Bake cookie crusts about 10 minutes or until lightly browned. Remove from oven and allow to cool completely. Remove each crust from the pan before filling.

In a mixing bowl, whisk together pudding mix and milk about five minutes or until thickened. Add a dollop of pudding mix to each cooled cookie crust. Refrigerate mini pies at least 30 minutes to firm them up.

While these are in the fridge, add coconut to a clean, dry skillet and toast for about 3 or 4 minutes. Remove mini pies from fridge and garnish with a little toasted coconut.

Hawaiian Shortcakes

If you can't get to Hawaii this year, you can certainly bring the flavors to your dessert. I cubed pieces of pound cake for this version, but you can use cubed pieces of angel food cake too.

INGREDIENTS

1 pound cake, cubed into bite-sized pieces

1 (16 ounce) container of Cool Whip, defrosted just a little bit

1 (15 ounce) can crushed pineapple (no need to drain)

1½ cups macadamia nuts, lightly toasted

2 cups sweetened flaked coconut, lightly toasted

You can use either one large trifle dish or 10 to 12 individual dishes for assembling and serving.

Layer in your dish(es), cubed pound cake, a little bit of Cool Whip, a little pineapple, some macadamia nuts, a sprinkle of coconut and repeat three times.

Finish with a little more Cool Whip and a garnish of toasted coconut. I like to make my shortcakes 24 hours in advance. The longer they sit in the fridge, the better they are. I would recommend at least 4 hours in advance up to 24.

Strawberry Banana Pie

My Grandmother's Strawberry Banana Pie is my favorite pie. Ever. It's not only super simple, it's just so delicious. This is the perfect accompaniment to a pool party. Or any party. Or a lazy afternoon. This pie is good for breakfast. It's always good.

INGREDIENTS

1 prepared pie crust, baked and ready to go (I just use a Pillsbury crust and pop it into the oven)

1 (3 ounce) package cream cheese

Juice of 1 lemon

1½ cups sugar

1 large container Cool Whip, thawed a bit

2 bananas, sliced

Sliced strawberries to top (probably 10 or so)

In a medium sized bowl, combine cream cheese, lemon juice and sugar with a wooden spoon. Fold in Cool Whip. Lay sliced bananas across the bottom of cooked (and fully cooled) pie shell. Top banana slices with Cool Whip mixture. Lay sliced strawberries across the top. Refrigerate at least 12 hours (if not, the sugar won't dissolve and the pie will be grainy tasting). Slice and serve.

Lemon Whoopie Pies

Being the lemon lover that I am, a lemon whoopie pie just makes sense.

INGREDIENTS

1 box lemon cake mix

½ cup vegetable oil

2 eggs

¼ cup water

Lemon Frosting

Preheat oven to 350 degrees.

Combine cake mix, oil, eggs, and water in bowl.

Drop by 2 tablespoons onto lined cookie sheet (leave about an inch between each cookie). Bake 9-10 minutes. Cool on pan 5 minutes, move to wire rack, and cool 15 more minutes.

Take one cookie and place a tablespoon or so of store-bought frosting in the center. Press another cookie on top (this will spread frosting out to the edge).

Pink Lemonade Bars

What's the only thing that makes lemon taste better? Adding a little pink. There's just something about that pink lemonade combination that says happy spring!

INGREDIENTS

1 box lemon cake mix

4 eggs

1 stick melted butter

1 box powdered sugar (about 4 cups)

1 (8 ounce) package cream cheese, softened

1 tablespoon lemon zest

2 tablespoons lemon juice

Pink food coloring

Preheat oven to 350 degrees. Spray a 9 x 13 baking dish. Set aside.

In a mixing bowl, combine cake mix, 2 eggs, and melted butter. Spread in bottom of pan to form first layer. In a second bowl, beat with electric mixer powdered sugar, 2 more eggs, cream cheese, lemon zest and lemon juice until smooth. Mix in food coloring. Spread this layer on top of first layer.

Bake 35 to 40 minutes until edges are slightly brown and center set (it will still be slightly wobbly in the middle). Remove from oven and cool on counter 30 minutes, then refrigerate 2 hours up to 2 days.

Not the sun or summer alone,
but every hour and season
yields its tribute of delight.

~Ralph Waldo Emerson

JUNE

DINNER

Pineapple Guacamole Burgers

Spinach and Sundried Tomato Turkey
Burgers

Cheddar Beer Burgers

Meatloaf Burgers

Maple Mustard Dogs

Mexican Paninis

Sweet and Sour Grilled Chicken Tacos

Crispy Potatoes and Sausage

Roasted Tomato and Sausage Pasta

Grilled Pizza

BREAKFAST

Breakfast Joes

Strawberry Lemon Bread

DESSERT

Lemon Berry Cobbler

Peanut Butter Krispies Treats

Root Beer Bars

Watermelon Cupcakes

Strawberry Pudding Pie

Pineapple Guacamole Burgers

When we were in Hawaii, I ate a pineapple guacamole burger and decided right then and there that I had to create our own version the minute we got home. I was unaware until that day that avocado and pineapple are soul mates. Soul mates! And this guacamole doesn't have to be only a topping for burgers. Go ahead and dip some chips in there!

INGREDIENTS

1 pound ground beef

2 tablespoons steak seasoning

Pinches of salt and pepper

1 avocado

1 (8 ounce) can crushed pineapple, not drained

1 red onion, chopped

Burger buns

Preheat outdoor grill or indoor grill pan to medium-high.

In a mixing bowl, combine the ground beef with steak seasoning and a pinch or two of salt and pepper. Divide the meat into four sections and make four patties. Grill the patties for 6 to 8 minutes per side or until they are done to your liking.

Meanwhile, in a mixing bowl, mash the avocado and combine it with the crushed pineapple (do not drain). Stir in the red onion and add a big pinch of salt.

Remove the burger patties from the grill and add to the buns. Top each patty with pineapple guacamole and serve.

Spinach and Sundried Tomato Turkey Burgers

I love having fancy burgers on a weeknight. Plus, with this recipe you're eating veggies you can mix and match inside! Don't forget, you need to clean your leeks! Leeks are grown in sandy soil, so chop them into bite-sized pieces, put them in a colander, and run lots of cold water over them. Lightly pat them dry with a paper towel.

INGREDIENTS

1 pound ground turkey (or chicken)

4 cloves garlic, grated

2 to 3 tablespoons extra virgin olive oil

1 package frozen spinach, thawed and drained of excess water

1/2 cup sundried tomatoes in oil, drained and chopped up a bit

2 teaspoons lemon zest

Salt and pepper

2 cups chopped leeks (or red onion, chopped)

1/2 cup feta cheese, crumbled

Burger buns

Preheat the outdoor grill or indoor grill pan to medium-high heat.

Combine the turkey, garlic, olive oil, spinach, tomatoes, lemon zest, and a liberal amount of salt and pepper in a mixing bowl. Divide the mixture into 4 burger patties.

Meanwhile, add a little more olive oil to a large skillet over medium heat and sauté the leeks or red onion with a little salt and pepper, until tender (about 15 minutes).

Place each burger patty on the grill and cook for about 8 minutes on each side. Remove the burgers from the grill when they're cooked through. Top each burger bun with one burger patty, a sprinkle of feta cheese, and some sautéed leeks.

Cheddar Beer Burgers

I love how beer brings flavor to a recipe. A dark beer works best here, but use what you have. And yes, all the alcohol will cook out so you can serve these burgers to your minors too. They will love them, so fire up your grill!

INGREDIENTS

1 pound ground beef

2/3 cup beer, divided

Pinch of salt and pepper

1 onion, chopped

Drizzle of extra virgin olive oil

1 tablespoon Dijon mustard

1 slice Cheddar cheese per burger

Burger buns

Preheat the outdoor grill to medium-high or preheat the indoor grill pan.

Combine the ground beef, 1/3 cup beer, and a liberal pinch of salt and pepper. Separate the meat mixture into four sections and shape each section into a patty. Grill the patties for about 6 minutes on each side or until they are done to your liking.

Meanwhile, in a large skillet over medium-high heat, sauté the onion in a drizzle of olive oil. Once the onions start to caramelize (in 5 minutes or so), stir in the Dijon mustard and 1/3 cup beer. Reduce the heat to low and let the onions sauté until the burgers are done (just a few minutes).

Top each burger with a slice of cheese about a minute before you pull them off the grill. Place a burger patty on each bun and top with onions.

Meatloaf Burgers

One of the reasons my Mom's Meatloaf is Andrew's very favorite meal is the yummy sauce. He loves it! And that sauce drizzled on basic burgers is delicious too. Just a simple little something extra. And since onions are in the meatloaf, I garnish our burgers with onions as well. Happy grilling!

INGREDIENTS

1 pound ground beef	⅔ cup brown sugar
2 tablespoons steak seasoning	1 teaspoon mustard
2 tablespoons Worcestershire Sauce	Burger buns
1 cup ketchup	Chopped green onions to garnish

Preheat the outdoor grill or the indoor grill pan to medium-high.

Combine the ground beef and steak seasoning, then divide the mixture into four burger patties.

Grill each patty about 5 or 6 minutes on each side or until they are cooked well enough for you.

Meanwhile, over a burner, heat the Worcestershire sauce, ketchup, brown sugar, and mustard in a small saucepan over medium heat. Heat the mixture through for about 5 minutes, stirring to make sure all the ingredients are incorporated. Remove the burgers from the grill and top with sauce.

Garnish with onions and serve on buns.

Maple Mustard Dogs

During the summer, hot dogs are a go-to dinner option for my little family. But I just can't eat the same dog all the time. I need a little switch-up! Here's a quick maple mustard sauce to drizzle on turkey or beef dogs, or brats. It will give you a delicious switch for a simple supper.

INGREDIENTS

1 onion, chopped	3 tablespoons maple syrup
Drizzle of extra virgin olive oil	(good quality!)
Pinches of salt and pepper	4 to 6 hot dogs, any kind
½ cup Dijon mustard	Hot dog buns

In a skillet over medium-high heat, sauté the onions in a drizzle of olive oil and a pinch of salt and pepper. Reduce the heat to low and let the onions caramelize for about 10 minutes.

Meanwhile, in a small bowl, combine the Dijon mustard and maple syrup with a pinch of salt and pepper. Reserve.

Grill the hot dogs over medium-high heat until they are warmed through (5 to 8 minutes). Serve each hot dog in a bun topped with caramelized onions and a drizzle of maple mustard sauce.

Mexican Paninis

My favorite part about these paninis is the chili cream cheese inside. If you don't have a panini press, place the panini in a skillet over medium-high heat and set another heavy skillet right on top of your sandwich to smush it down. Cook for 3 to 4 minutes, flip the sandwich, and cook for another 3 to 4 minutes.

INGREDIENTS

1 (3 ounce) package cream cheese, softened

2 tablespoons chili powder

1 onion, sliced

2 bell peppers, sliced (I use one yellow and one red)

1 tablespoon extra virgin olive oil

Salt and pepper

Salsa (for dipping)

1 loaf sourdough bread, sliced

1 pound cooked fajita beef, chopped (I buy it pre-cooked)

1 cup Monterey Jack cheese, shredded

Preheat a panini press or large skillet. Lightly spray with cooking spray.

In a small bowl, combine the cream cheese and chili powder with a spoon. Set aside.

In a skillet over medium-high heat, sauté the onion and bell peppers in 1 tablespoon of olive oil and a little salt and pepper for about 5 to 6 minutes.

Take two slices of bread, and spread the chili cream cheese on each one. Then on one of the slices, place beef, bell peppers, and onions, and sprinkle with cheese. Top with the second slice of bread. Place the sandwich under the panini press for about 5 minutes or until golden and the cheese is melted. Slice the sandwich in half and serve with your favorite salsa for dipping.

Sweet and Sour Grilled Chicken Tacos

I took the flavors of Sweet and Sour Chicken and turned it into a taco. Instead of using cornstarch and whipping up a traditional sweet and sour sauce, I made a marinade out of it, grilled up our chicken, and topped it with a pineapple salsa. I use rice wine vinegar and Hoisin Sauce because I keep them on hand at my house. If you do not (and do not wish to purchase them), you can substitute apple cider vinegar and/or BBQ sauce.

INGREDIENTS

1 tablespoon brown sugar

¼ cup rice wine vinegar (you can substitute apple cider vinegar)

1 (15 ounce) can pineapple chunks, divided

1 pound of boneless skinless chicken breasts

1 red bell pepper, cut into chunks

8 green onions, chopped

2 tablespoons Hoisin sauce (or BBQ sauce)

8 lightly toasted taco shells

In a pie plate or large mixing bowl, whisk together the brown sugar, vinegar, and the juice of your canned pineapple (reserving the chunks!). Add in chicken breasts and coat in the mixture. Cover with plastic wrap and refrigerate at least 30 minutes or up to 12 hours.

Preheat your grill to medium-high heat and when you're ready, remove chicken from fridge, drain and discard the marinade, and grill your chicken (about 8 minutes or so per side). Grill until the chicken is cooked completely and the juices run clear when the skin is pierced.

While the chicken is grilling, make pineapple salsa. Toss together in a small bowl pineapple chunks, chopped red bell pepper, green onions (reserving a few onions for garnish), and Hoisin sauce.

Once chicken is grilled to perfection, remove and slice into strips. Assemble tacos with grilled chicken, pineapple salsa, and a few extra green onions.

Crispy Potatoes and Sausage

I love dinners like this. It's a simple meat-and-potato meal, and in spring and summer we love a sausage supper. (My kiddos love this because, in their little world, it's pretty much a hot dog and French fries.) I use spicy jalapeño chicken sausages and mild Italian turkey sausages, but you can use whatever you like. Your family will love it!

INGREDIENTS

8 sausage links, any variety

8 Yukon Gold potatoes (or red potatoes)

1 tablespoon Dijon mustard

⅓ cup extra virgin olive oil, plus a little more for the tomatoes

2 tablespoons Parmesan cheese, grated

Pinches of salt and pepper

Parsley to garnish

8 asparagus stalks

1 pint cherry tomatoes

For the sausages: You can either grill the sausages or cook them in a hot skillet or grill pan on the stove over medium-high heat. Heat them until they are cooked through and crispy on the sides. I cook mine on the grill pan for about 10 minutes. Pierce the middle of the sausages to make sure they have been cooked through and the juices run clear.

For the potatoes: Preheat the oven to 425 degrees. Line a baking sheet with foil and lightly spray with cooking spray for easy cleanup. Set aside.

Chop each potato into bite-sized pieces. Set aside.

In a mixing bowl, add the Dijon mustard and then whisk ⅓ cup olive oil into the bowl. Stir in the Parmesan cheese.

Toss the potatoes into the mustard mixture and then spread them out on the prepared baking sheet. Sprinkle salt and pepper over the potatoes and then roast them for about 45 minutes. Halfway through the baking time, toss the potatoes around to make sure all sides get nice and crispy. When the potatoes are nice and crispy, remove them from the oven and garnish them with a little chopped parsley.

For the roasted veggies: Preheat the oven to 425 degrees. Line a baking sheet with foil and lightly spray with cooking spray for easy cleanup. Spread the chopped asparagus (I chop the stalks in thirds) and the entire pint of cherry tomatoes over the baking sheet. Drizzle 1 to 2 tablespoons of olive oil over the top of everything. Add a liberal pinch of salt and pepper to the veggies. Roast them in the oven for about 15 minutes before removing and serving.

Roasted Tomato and Sausage Pasta

You can mix and match this recipe a million different ways—omit, add, change. The pasta is ready in no time and is sure to get your family eating loads of healthy veggies. You can also add a cup packaged sundried tomatoes instead of roasting tomatoes, but roasted tomatoes are so delicious that I highly recommend making them! Yum, yum, yum!

INGREDIENTS

1 pint grape or cherry tomatoes (or 1 cup packaged sundried tomatoes)

1 tablespoon extra virgin olive oil, plus more for drizzling

Pinches of salt and pepper

1 pound pasta (I use whole wheat rigatoni)

1 pound pork sausage (or chicken sausage or turkey sausage)

3 to 4 cloves garlic, chopped

1 cup chicken broth

1 package chopped frozen spinach, thawed and drained of excess water

Freshly grated Parmesan cheese, as much or as little as your family likes

4 to 5 basil leaves, chopped

1 tablespoon butter (optional)

To roast tomatoes: Preheat the oven to 425 degrees. Line a baking sheet with foil and lightly spray with cooking spray; spread cherry tomatoes on baking sheet. Drizzle 1 to 2 tablespoons of olive oil over the top and sprinkle liberally with salt and pepper. Roast the tomatoes in the oven for about 15 minutes.

To make pasta: Bring one large pot of water to a boil. Drop the pasta and cook until al dente.

In another pan, heat 1 tablespoon of olive oil over medium-high heat and brown the sausage. Once the sausage is brown, add the garlic and sauté a minute. Once the sausage and garlic are both browned, pour in the chicken broth to deglaze the pan (scrape the little bits off the bottom). Lower heat to low and let the chicken broth simmer for 2 to 3 minutes. Add the thawed spinach and tomatoes. Stir for 2 to 3 minutes, allowing the spinach to heat through.

Drain the pasta and add to the sausage pan. Stir in the cheese and basil. You can also stir in 1 tablespoon of butter now to give this dish a little something extra.

Grilled Pizza

Grilling pizza outside is great—as long as you make it while you can still stand the summer heat! I slice chicken sausage into rounds and cook them in a skillet with a splash of olive oil for about 10 minutes before putting them on the pizza. Also, trust me, a pizza stone is a must. But do not preheat your outdoor grill. The stone needs to be placed on a cold grill or it will crack.

INGREDIENTS

Pizza dough (homemade or store-bought)

1 (10 ounce) jar pizza sauce

1 cup mozzarella cheese, shredded

1 cup Italian blend cheese, shredded

2 cups spinach leaves (I buy bagged spinach)

1 cup pepperoni (optional, but we like turkey pepperoni along with the sausage)

1 cup basil leaves, torn into big pieces, not finely chopped

1 pound sausage, cut into rounds and already cooked

Roll out the dough on pizza stone. Top the dough with all the ingredients in the order given above. Place the pizza stone on your outdoor grill and turn on to medium heat. Close the lid of the grill and cook for about 15 minutes, occasionally checking on the pizza. Once pizza is golden and bubbly, remove from the grill. Slice and serve!

Breakfast Joes

It's no secret that we're sloppy joe people. We love us a joe for supper so much that I started making them for breakfast!

INGREDIENTS

½ pound breakfast sausage (I use 8 ounces of Owen's)

12 eggs or egg whites (or a combination of both)

a splash of milk, half and half, or cream

1 cup Monterey Jack cheese, shredded

3 or 4 tablespoons chives, snipped into pieces (plus more for garnish)

4 English muffins, toasted and split in half

Salt and pepper

Salsa for drizzling

Heat a large skillet over medium-high heat and brown sausage. While sausage is browning, beat eggs and milk in a bowl with a wire whisk. Add in a nice pinch of salt and pepper.

Once the sausage is browned and crumbly, lower the heat just a little under your skillet and pour your beaten eggs in the skillet on top of the sausage. Scramble your eggs and sausage together (it takes about 4 minutes or so). Once eggs are scrambled, stir in cheese and snipped chives.

To serve, lay out both halves of your English muffin on each plate and scoop the sausage and egg mixture over the top. Drizzle salsa on the eggs and a few more snipped pieces of chives.

Strawberry Lemon Bread

This recipe makes one loaf of bread but can easily be doubled for an extra loaf that will freeze beautifully. Just allow the frozen loaf to come to room temp on the kitchen counter when you're ready to enjoy.

INGREDIENTS

2 eggs

1 cup sugar

¾ cup vegetable oil

1 cup chopped strawberries

Juice and zest of one lemon
(about 2 tablespoons of juice and
1 tablespoon of zest)

1¼ cups flour

½ teaspoon baking soda

½ teaspoon salt

Preheat oven to 350 degrees. Lightly spray one loaf pan with cooking spray. Set aside.

In a large mixing bowl, beat eggs until light and frothy. Beat in sugar and oil. Beat in strawberries. Stir in lemon juice and zest. Set aside.

In a second mixing bowl, combine flour, baking soda, and salt and mix together with a fork.

Slowly beat flour mixture into strawberry mixture. Beat until just combined.

Pour batter into prepared pan and bake 45 to 55 minutes. A toothpick inserted in the center of the loaf should come out clean when the bread is done. Allow the bread to cool at least 20 minutes before removing it from the pan and slicing it.

Lemon Berry Cobbler

I can usually make sweets and treats, sample them, and then move on. But this dessert...I can eat the entire pan. All of it. Gone. It's simple, it's yummy, it's like everything I love in life in one bowl.

INGREDIENTS

1 (10 ounce) package frozen raspberries (or mixed berries, whichever you prefer!)

1 (21 ounce) can blackberry pie filling

1 lemon cake mix

1 stick butter, melted

Ice cream, optional

Preheat oven to 350 degrees. Grease a 9 x 13 baking dish.

Spread frozen berries across the bottom of baking dish. Next, spoon pie filling on top of the frozen berries and then sprinkle the dry cake mix over top. Finally, drizzle the melted butter over everything.

Bake uncovered 55 to 60 minutes.

Remove from oven and serve immediately (with a little ice cream if you so desire).

Peanut Butter Krispies Treats

This is the very first thing I learned how to make by myself. This little recipe right here. My grandmother always made these for us when we would go swimming at her house. To this day, every time we have a family pool party, someone brings these. Every time. I was eight the first time I made these and I've probably made them 10,000 times since. These are so simple and yet so incredibly delicious.

INGREDIENTS

1 cup sugar

1 cup light corn syrup

1 cup creamy peanut butter

6 cups Rice Krispies cereal

In a small saucepan over medium-high heat, bring sugar and corn syrup up to a boil, stirring continuously. Once to a low boil, remove from heat and stir in peanut butter. Pour peanut butter mixture over 6 cups of cereal in a large mixing bowl. Combine quickly until cereal is covered and then spread out into a well-greased 8 x 8 baking dish. Cool at least 10 minutes before cutting into squares.

Root Beer Bars

Chocolate brownie-like bars with a creamy root beer frosting... Yup, this does it for me. My kiddos loved it, I loved it, and I'm pretty sure you'll love it too.

INGREDIENTS

1 box chocolate cake mix

½ cup vegetable oil

2 eggs

1 cup chocolate chips

1 stick butter, softened

3 cups powdered sugar

2 to 3 tablespoons root beer

Preheat oven to 350 degrees. Grease a 9 x 13 baking dish. Set aside.

In a large mixing bowl, combine cake mix, vegetable oil, and eggs with an electric mixer until creamy. Stir in chocolate chips. Pour batter into prepared baking dish and bake about 10 minutes or until a toothpick inserted into the middle comes out mostly clean (do not over bake).

Remove from oven and cool completely before frosting.

To make the frosting, beat your butter, powdered sugar, and root beer with an electric mixer. Add more powdered sugar if it's too thin or more root beer if it's too thick.

Frost cooled bars and store in the fridge when you're not enjoying.

Watermelon Cupcakes

I puree fresh watermelon in my blender but you can also buy frozen watermelon in the freezer department (it comes in a liquid form ready for smoothies) and defrost that too. No matter how you get your watermelon, you are going to love these delicious cupcakes.

INGREDIENTS

1 box white cake mix

1¼ cups pureed watermelon, divided

½ cup vegetable oil

4 egg whites

Pink food coloring, optional

½ cup butter, softened

2 cups powdered sugar

Preheat oven to 350 degrees. Line 2 (12-count) muffin tins with paper liners. Set aside.

In a large mixing bowl, beat white cake mix, 1 cup pureed watermelon, vegetable oil, and egg whites with an electric mixer. Beat in a drop or two of pink food coloring.

Pour batter into prepared muffin tins and bake 19 to 21 minutes or until a toothpick inserted in the middle comes out clean. Allow cupcakes to cool in tin about 10 minutes before removing them to wire racks to finish cooling.

Meanwhile, in a mixing bowl, beat butter, remaining ¼ cup pureed watermelon, and powdered sugar until blended. Add more watermelon if the frosting is too thick or more sugar if it's too thin. Beat in a drop or two of pink food coloring.

Frost cooled cupcakes with Watermelon Frosting. Store in the refrigerator when not enjoying.

Strawberry Pudding Pie

This time of year, I'm always trying to come up with recipes that are perfect for patio dining and swim parties. I love pies like this because you make them in advance, pop them in the fridge, and then slice and serve when you're ready to eat. Plus, when strawberries are in season ... this pie is just extra fabulous. So simple, so seasonal, so strawberry. Enjoy!

INGREDIENTS

1 (5 ounce) box instant vanilla pudding (do not prepare!)

4 ounces cream cheese, softened (half a package)

1 (14 ounce) can sweetened condensed milk

2$\frac{1}{2}$ cups chopped strawberries (plus a few for garnish)

1 pie crust, baked and ready to be filled

Whipped cream for garnish

In a large mixing bowl, beat unprepared vanilla pudding mix, cream cheese, and sweetened condensed milk with an electric mixer until just combined. Stir in your chopped strawberries. Pour pie filling into your prepared pie crust and refrigerate at least four hours up to 24 hours. When you're ready to serve, slice into wedges and garnish with a little whipped cream and an additional strawberry.

*A life without love is
like a year without summer.*

~Swedish Proverb

JULY

DINNER

Caprese Turkey Burgers

Spinach and Sundried
Tomato Joes

Taco Burgers

Green Chile Cheeseburgers

Tomatillo and Pineapple Burgers

Honey Mustard and
Lime Chicken Tostadas

Enchilada Suizas

Chipotle Fish Tacos

Quick Chicken Stir-Fry

Sweet Onion and Asparagus Pasta

BREAKFAST

Blueberry French Toast Bake

Strawberry Muffins

DESSERT

Strawberry Angel Food Cake

Lemon Coconut Bars

Strawberry Cupcakes with Blueberry
Cream Cheese Frosting

Red, White, and Blue Trifle

Banana Pudding

Caprese Turkey Burgers

I just love Caprese salad. You know, basil, fresh mozzarella, and tomatoes. I love it so much that I decided to make a burger that tastes like one. Honestly, this burger is just about as simple as assembling a boring old plain burger, but with a lot more flavor—and a few hidden veggies too! Before you know it, dinner is ready, and it's really, really good!

INGREDIENTS

1 pint cherry tomatoes

2 tablespoons extra virgin olive oil

Salt and pepper

1 pound ground turkey

1 box chopped frozen spinach, thawed and drained of excess water

4 thick slices of fresh mozzarella

Basil leaves to garnish

Burger buns

Preheat the oven to 400 degrees. Spread the tomatoes on a baking sheet lined with foil for easy cleanup. Drizzle about 2 tablespoons of olive oil over the tops of the tomatoes and add a liberal amount of salt and pepper. Roast the tomatoes for about 15 minutes.

While the tomatoes are roasting, make the burgers. In a medium-sized bowl, combine the ground turkey and spinach. Form the turkey mixture into four burger patties. On the outside grill or indoor grill pan, cook the burgers about 8 minutes per side over medium-high heat. Remove the cooked patties from the grill and assemble the burgers. Top each bun with a patty, a slice of fresh mozzarella, some roasted tomatoes, and a few basil leaves. Then drizzle everything with a bit of olive oil and a pinch of salt and pepper.

Spinach and Sundried Tomato Joes

My love affair with the sloppy joe and sundried tomatoes led me to combine them for a simple, flavorful, and delicious supper. Such a fun twist on a yummy meatball recipe!

INGREDIENTS

1 pound ground turkey

Salt and pepper

4 cloves garlic, minced

1 package frozen spinach, thawed and drained of excess water

1 (8 ounce) jar sundried tomatoes in oil, drained

2 teaspoons lemon zest

Feta cheese, crumbled to garnish

Green onions, chopped to garnish

Extra virgin olive oil

Burger buns

In a large skillet over medium-high heat, brown the turkey in a drizzle of olive oil until browned and crumbly. Add a liberal pinch of salt and pepper. Stir in the garlic, spinach, sundried tomatoes, and lemon zest. Reduce the heat to medium and let simmer for about 5 minutes or until everything is heated through.

Top each burger bun with a generous portion of ground turkey mixture. Garnish with feta cheese and chopped green onions.

Taco Burgers

This is just the best idea ever. We make burgers that taste like tacos, and they are flippin' fabulous! Next time it's Taco Night at your house, make these taco burgers instead! They are such a fun twist on a traditional burger, and easy to make too!

INGREDIENTS

1 pound ground beef

2 tablespoons chili powder or taco seasoning

Pinches of salt and pepper

4 slices Monterey Jack cheese

Burger buns

Salsa to drizzle on each burger

1 avocado, sliced

Deli-sliced jalapeños and chopped green onion to garnish

Preheat the outdoor grill or the indoor grill pan to medium-high.

In a mixing bowl, combine the ground beef with chili powder or taco seasoning and a pinch or two of salt and pepper. Divide the meat into four sections and make four patties.

Grill the burger patties for 6 to 8 minutes per side, or until they are done to your liking. Add 1 slice of cheese to each burger about a minute before you pull them off the grill. Remove the burger patties from the grill and add to buns. Top each patty with a little salsa, a slice of avocado, some jalapeños, and some green onions.

Green Chile Cheeseburgers

When we have a long summer still ahead of us, I can't be eating the same old burger week after week. I have to spice it up a bit! These Green Chile Cheeseburgers are super simple and super yummy, so fire up the grill! You can even serve them on tortillas or tostada shells.

INGREDIENTS

1½ pounds ground beef	Pepper Jack cheese
1 packet taco seasoning	Guacamole, salsa, and/or sour cream
1 (4 ounce) can chopped green chilies	Burger buns

Preheat the outdoor grill or indoor grill pan to medium-high.

In a mixing bowl, combine the ground beef, taco seasoning, and green chilies. Once incorporated, divide the meat into four sections and create four burger patties.

Grill the burger patties for 6 to 7 minutes per side (a little longer for a more well-done burger). Sprinkle cheese over the burgers the last minute they're on the grill. Remove the burgers from the grill and add one to each burger bun. Top with guacamole, salsa, and/or sour cream.

Tomatillo and Pineapple Burgers

I love coming up with easy and flavorful new ways to make my weeknight burger feel more special. The sweetness of the pineapple in this recipe pairs well with the spiciness of jalapeño and the cheese. And though I use my homemade version of this salsa, you can make a quick, store-bought version: buy a jar of tomatillo salsa and combine it with crushed pineapple.

INGREDIENTS

8 to 10 tomatillos, husks removed and rinsed off	1½ pounds ground beef
3 to 4 cloves garlic	2 tablespoons steak seasoning (or whatever seasoning blend you have that pairs nicely with beef)
1 onion, sliced	
1 jalapeño pepper, sliced (remove seeds for a less spicy version)	Salt and pepper
	Pepper Jack cheese slices
Juice of one lime	Burger buns
1 (8 ounce) can pineapple tidbits or crushed pineapple, drained	1 avocado, sliced

To make the salsa: In the bowl of your food processor, combine the tomatillos, garlic, onion, jalapeño, and lime juice, and pulse until salsa consistency. Stir in the pineapple. Refrigerate until you're ready to eat.

To make the burgers: Preheat the outdoor grill or the indoor grill pan to medium-high. In a medium-sized mixing bowl, combine the ground beef with steak seasoning and a little salt and pepper. Divide the ground beef mixture into four burger patties. Grill for about 6 minutes on each side. Add a slice of cheese on top about a minute before they're done.

To assemble your burgers: Top one bun with a burger patty, sliced avocado, and then your tomatillo-pineapple salsa.

Serve open-faced.

Honey Mustard and Lime Chicken Tostadas

This dinner was inspired by tortilla chips I had at a Mexican food restaurant in Joplin, Missouri. They had the best tortilla chips I've ever eaten (and I'm a Texas girl; I eat a ton of tortilla chips!). They were crispy and covered in salt and lime juice, and I decided to create a dinner around the lime juice and chip concept. It was a hit! And this isn't even cooking; it's assembling!

INGREDIENTS

1½ pounds cooked chicken, chopped

¾ cup honey mustard salad dressing

⅓ cup tomatillo salsa

1 red onion, diced

Monterey Jack cheese, shredded

2 limes

Tostada shells

In a medium-sized bowl, combine the shredded cooked chicken, honey mustard dressing, and salsa. Top each tostada shell with some chicken mixture, then top with red onion and shredded cheese. Finally, squeeze a wedge of lime juice over the top of each tostada.

Enchilada Suizas

Enchilada Suizas are a chicken enchilada with Swiss cheese inside. I used to think enchiladas were too much of a hassle for a weeknight, but I was wrong. They're actually the perfect weeknight supper and an easy recipe to whip up if you need to take someone dinner or a dish to a potluck.

INGREDIENTS

1 pound cooked and shredded chicken

1 can cream of mushroom soup

1 (4 ounce) can chopped green chilies

Salt and pepper

1 cup Swiss cheese, shredded (save a little extra for garnish)

½ cup Pepper Jack cheese, shredded (or Monterey Jack)

8 tortillas (either flour or whole wheat)

1 (15 ounce) can tomatillo or green chili enchilada sauce

Chopped green onions to garnish

Preheat oven to 400 degrees. Lightly spray an 8 x 8 baking dish with cooking spray. Set aside.

In a large mixing bowl, combine the shredded chicken with the cream of mushroom soup, green chilies, a liberal pinch of salt and pepper, and both cheeses.

Once combined, take each tortilla and spread a little bit down the center. Roll and place in the prepared baking dish. Once all 8 enchiladas are tucked inside the baking dish, pour your enchilada sauce on top of them.

Bake uncovered about 20 minutes or until the edges of the tortillas are lightly brown and everything is bubbling. Remove from oven and serve. Garnish with some chopped green onion and a little extra Swiss.

Chipotle Fish Tacos

We used cod for these grilled fish tacos but any nice firm white fish will do. The spicy fish fillets next to the creamy slaw are just so good! This is the kind of recipe you will make over and over again this summer.

INGREDIENTS

For the fish:

4 (6 to 8 ounce) cod fish fillets

1 Tablespoon Old Bay Seasoning

1 (7 ounce) can chipotle peppers in adobo sauce

Juice of one lemon

Large flour tortillas for serving

For the slaw:

¼ cup real mayonnaise

1 tablespoon apple cider vinegar

½ tablespoon sugar

Pinch salt and pepper

4 cups shredded purple cabbage

Optional garnish:

2 avocados smashed with a fork

Lemon wedges

Preheat outdoor grill or indoor grill pan to medium heat.

In a mixing bowl, whisk together the mayonnaise, vinegar, sugar, salt, and pepper. Add in purple cabbage and coat everything in mixture. Cover and refrigerate at least 10 minutes (up to an hour).

Next, take each fish fillet and lay it out. Sprinkle Old Bay Seasoning (or a bit of salt and pepper) over both sides of each fillet. Set aside.

Remove two chipotle peppers from the can and chop them up (the adobo sauce will be on them and that's okay!). The chopped peppers will almost make like a paste on your cutting board. Spread a little of this chipotle mixture on each side of each fillet. Chop another pepper if you need more (several peppers are in each can).

Slice your lemon in half and squirt a little lemon over the tops of each fillet before taking them to the grill.

Grill up each side of your fish (about 4 or 5 minutes per side).

Remove from grill and assemble your tacos: tortilla, slaw, fish, a little mashed up avocado, and a little wedge of lemon.

Quick Chicken Stir-Fry

It's funny. If I put boring old veggies in front of my kiddos they'll turn up their noses. But if I stick them in a stir-fry they'll eat them up. Here is a really quick way to get a stir-fry on your table on a busy weeknight. I use a red onion, red bell pepper, sugar snap peas, and broccoli, but mix and match any veggies you like. You'll need at least one cup veggies per person.

INGREDIENTS

4 tablespoons sesame seeds

1 tablespoon extra virgin olive oil

1½ pounds skinless chicken breasts, boneless and cut into bite-sized pieces

Salt and pepper

4 cups veggies (any variety you like)

1 (5 ounce) bottle soy sauce, divided

Prepared white or brown rice ready for serving

Juice of 1 orange (about ½ cup)

2 teaspoons Dijon mustard

Add the seeds to a dry skillet over medium-high heat and brown them for about 2 minutes. Remove from the heat and reserve.

Preheat a griddle, wok, or large skillet over high heat. Add 1 tablespoon of olive oil. Add the chicken breasts and season with salt and pepper. Brown the chicken on all sides (about 8 minutes).

Reduce the heat to medium-high and add the veggies. Add another pinch of salt and pepper. Once the veggies begin to get tender, toss everything together with about half the bottle of soy sauce (several big tablespoons). Remove from the heat and top the prepared rice with chicken, veggies, and toasted sesame seeds.

We like a little orange Dijon sauce with ours, so in a small bowl, I whisk together orange juice, Dijon mustard, and 2 tablespoons of soy sauce. The sauce is perfect for drizzling.

Sweet Onion and Asparagus Pasta

The beauty of this recipe is that you can mix and match any veggies that look good to you—bell pepper, zucchini, cherry tomatoes, or whatever you have or like. (One night Andrew and Kensington came home from the grocery store with a big sweet onion, asparagus, and mushrooms for my pasta!) We use a sweet Italian chicken sausage, but any sausage will provide a great flavor.

INGREDIENTS

1 pound short-cut pasta (I use penne)

1 tablespoon extra virgin olive oil

1 pound sausage

1 large sweet onion, chopped

1 clove garlic, chopped

1 big handful mushrooms, chopped (any variety)

2 cups chicken stock

1 cup Parmesan cheese, grated and divided

10 to 12 asparagus, chopped into bite-sized pieces

Splash of milk, cream, or half-and-half

Salt and pepper

Parsley to garnish

Bring a large pot of water to a boil over medium-high heat. Drop the pasta and cook to al dente (6 to 7 minutes).

Meanwhile, in a large skillet over medium-high heat, drizzle 1 tablespoon of olive oil. Add the sausage and brown. Once the sausage is browned and crumbly, add the chopped onion and sauté for a few minutes until soft. Add the garlic and mushrooms and sauté for a few more minutes. Stir in the chicken stock and deglaze the pan (scrape the little bits off the bottom). Stir in the Parmesan and asparagus and reduce heat to low. Simmer for about 5 minutes. Stir in the milk and a nice pinch of salt and pepper.

Drain the pasta and add it to the skillet of sausage. Stir to incorporate. Garnish with parsley and more Parmesan, and serve.

Blueberry French Toast Bake

Is there anything better than a breakfast casserole? I mean a piece of this with a cup coffee and I am one happy lady. I love that I can make this the night before and then just pop it in the oven the following morning.

INGREDIENTS

1 loaf of bread (about 4 cups of cubed pieces) torn into bite-size pieces (I use Challah but you could use croissants too)

6 eggs

1½ cups milk

1½ cups half-and-half

1 teaspoon vanilla extract

1 teaspoon cinnamon

2 cups fresh blueberries

Maple syrup to drizzle on top, optional

Arrange bread in a lightly greased 9 x 13 baking pan; set aside. Whisk eggs, milk, half and half, vanilla, and cinnamon in a mixing bowl; pour over bread. Sprinkle blueberries down over the top. Cover and refrigerate overnight.

The next morning, preheat oven to 350 degrees and bake 45 to 55 minutes. (Check after about 30 minutes and if it's getting too brown on top, cover with foil and continue cooking.) Remove from oven and let stand 5 minutes before serving. You can drizzle maple syrup over top if you like.

Strawberry Muffins

I'm not opposed to muffins out of a box (I love them actually!), but sometimes I want one from scratch. But when I say scratch, I mean easy enough to whip up with two toddlers sitting on the kitchen counter helping. This recipe fits the bill.

INGREDIENTS

1½ cups strawberries, chopped

¾ cup sugar, divided

¼ cup butter, softened

2 eggs

1 teaspoon vanilla

1¾ cups flour

½ teaspoon baking soda

½ teaspoon salt

1 teaspoon cinnamon

Preheat oven to 425 degrees. Line a 12-cup muffin tin with liners. Combine strawberries and ½ cup sugar in a bowl and let it sit together at least one hour (this will allow the strawberries to get all juicy and yummy).

In a mixing bowl, cream together butter and remaining ¼ cup sugar until fluffy. Slowly beat in eggs one at a time. Stir in vanilla. In a separate bowl, combine the flour, baking soda, salt, and cinnamon. Slowly stir flour mixture into butter mixture until incorporated. Fold in strawberries and all the liquid from the reserved bowl. Spoon into prepared muffin tin.

Bake 18 to 20 minutes or until toothpick inserted in the middle comes out clean. Allow to rest in pan 5 to 10 minutes before removing.

Strawberry Angel Food Cake

This is my two-ingredient Strawberry Angel Food cake (okay, three if you count the dollop of Cool Whip). My dad loves strawberry shortcake and so I bought the ingredients to make it one evening when they were coming to dinner. But I decided at the last minute that I was bored with plain old strawberry shortcake and wondered what would happen if instead of using water in the angel food cake mixture, I used the strawberries instead. What happened was magic. This is so good and so easy. You'll probably never go back to boring old strawberry shortcake again.

INGREDIENTS

1 box angel food cake mix

Cool Whip

Sweetened frozen strawberries, thawed (read cake box to determine how much to use)

Preheat oven to 350 degrees. Pour cake mix into a bowl. Instead of using the amount of water per your box directions, substitute the strawberries and juice. (Measure it out in a measuring cup. It's fine if pieces of strawberry fall in.) Beat with an electric mixer until combined, about one minute. Your batter will turn nice and pink while mixing.

Pour into a greased 9 x 13 glass baking dish and bake about 30 minutes. Remove from oven when a toothpick inserted in the middle comes out dry. Let cake rest on counter about 20 minutes before slicing.

Slice and serve with a heaping dollop of Cool Whip.

Lemon Coconut Bars

This is it! This is the bar you will make over and over again this spring and summer. You'll make it once, everyone will love it, and then you'll keep making it for every occasion between now and Labor Day. This is your new favorite bar.

INGREDIENTS

1 box lemon cake mix

4 eggs

1 stick melted butter

1 box powdered sugar (about 4 cups)

1 (8 ounce) package cream cheese, softened

2 cups sweetened flaked coconut

Preheat oven to 350 degrees. Grease one 9 x 13 baking pan.

In a mixing bowl, combine cake mix, 2 eggs, and melted butter. Spread in bottom of pan.

In a second bowl, beat with electric mixer powdered sugar, 2 more eggs, and cream cheese. Stir in your coconut. Spread coconut mixture on top of crust mixture.

Bake 35 to 40 minutes until edges are brown and center set (it will still be slightly wobbly in the middle).

Cool on counter 30 minutes, then refrigerate 2 hours or up to 2 days. Slice into bars and serve.

Strawberry Cupcakes with Blueberry Cream Cheese Frosting

Red, white, and yummy all over, your friends and family will love these cupcakes!

INGREDIENTS

1 box strawberry cake mix

3 egg whites

1/2 cup vegetable oil

1 1/4 cups water

1 cup chopped fresh strawberries

1 (8 ounce) package cream cheese, softened

2 cups powdered sugar

1 cup blueberries

1 tablespoon milk or cream

Preheat oven to 350 degrees.

Line 2 (12 count) muffin tins with cupcake liners. Set aside.

In a large mixing bowl, beat cake mix, egg whites, vegetable oil, and water with an electric mixer. Once combined, stir in chopped strawberries.

Fill each cupcake liner 2/3 full with batter and bake in the oven about 18 minutes or until a toothpick inserted in the middle comes out clean. Remove cupcakes from oven and allow to cool in the pans 10 minutes before removing them to a wire rack to finish cooling.

While the cupcakes are cooling, make frosting. In a mixing bowl, beat cream cheese with the powdered sugar and a splash of milk. Add more powdered sugar if the frosting is too thin and more milk if it's too thick. Once the frosting reaches your desired consistency, stir in fresh blueberries.

Top each cooled cupcake with frosting and enjoy! Refrigerate cupcakes when storing.

Red, White, and Blue Trifle

Every year on the Fourth of July, we have some sort of strawberry and blueberry dessert because it looks all fun and patriotic. This year, I took angel food cake from my grocery store's bakery and turned our annual treat into a trifle. Burgers, swimming, fireworks, watermelon, and this dessert are all you need on your Fourth.

INGREDIENTS

1 large box (5 ounce) instant vanilla pudding

1 can sweetened condensed milk

½ cup water

1 large (12 ounce) Cool Whip, thawed

1 (8 ounce) container sour cream

1 angel food cake, cut into big pieces

About 2 cups fresh strawberries, sliced

About one cup blueberries

In a large bowl, combine pudding, milk, and water with a whisk. Refrigerate this mixture 5 minutes. Remove from fridge and stir in Cool Whip and sour cream until smooth.

In a large trifle dish (or individual dishes), layer angel food cake across the bottom, add a layer of strawberry slices and a few blueberries over the cake then add ⅓ of your pudding mixture. Repeat 3 times. Finish off with a few more strawberries and blueberries on top to garnish.

Refrigerate at least 4 hours and up to 2 days before serving.

Banana Pudding

I have layered this pudding in mason jars, trifle dishes, big bowls...a multitude of things. Sometimes I make individual puddings and sometimes I make one big dessert in a large dish. It's your call. Warm nights and summer entertaining call for this dessert.

INGREDIENTS

1 large box instant vanilla pudding

3 cups milk

1 can Eagle Brand Milk

1 (12 ounce) Cool Whip, thawed a bit

1 box Nilla Wafer Cookies

2-3 bananas, sliced

In a mixing bowl, combine pudding and milk with a whisk. Then whisk in Eagle Brand Milk and Cool Whip. In your serving dish, layer cookies, a few banana slices, and some pudding mixture. Repeat until you reach the top. Keep refrigerated until you're ready to serve. (The longer it sits in the refrigerator, the better it becomes...sometimes as long as 3 days.)

August is like the
Sunday of summer.
~ANONYMOUS

AUGUST

DINNER

Brisket Ranch Sandwiches

Meatball Subs

BBQ Joes

Orange Marmalade Chicken Sandwiches

Cumin Crusted Chicken

Chipotle and Corn Chicken Waffles

Green Chile Chicken Baked Tacos

Pesto Quinoa and Chicken Stuffed Bell
Peppers

Peanut Pasta

Sausage Tortellini Bake

BREAKFAST

Blueberry Banana Bread

Nutella Cinnamon Rolls

DESSERT

Piña Colada Pie

Snickerdoodle Bars

PB&J Bars

Bananas Foster Trifle

Brisket Ranch Sandwiches

On a hot August day, it's nice not to heat up the kitchen with the stove and oven. Instead, I let my slow cooker do all the work!

INGREDIENTS

2 pound brisket (flat and trimmed)

1 (4 ounce) bottle liquid smoke (use either hickory or mesquite flavored)

4 cups beef stock

Extra virgin olive oil

Salt and pepper

A few handfuls of romaine lettuce

2 avocados, sliced

Ranch salad dressing

1 red onion, chopped

4 to 6 hoagie rolls, split in half

In a large pot over medium-high heat, brown both sides of the brisket in about two tablespoons of olive oil. Salt and pepper each side of the brisket quite liberally. After each side is browned (about 3 minutes per side) add brisket to slow cooker along with the entire bottle of liquid smoke and beef stock. Cover and cook on low about 8 hours or on high 4 hours.

When you're ready to assemble your sandwiches, remove brisket from slow cooker (discard all liquid) and slice it up on your cutting board. Take each dinner roll and top with Romaine lettuce, sliced brisket, several pieces of avocado, chopped red onion, and a drizzle of ranch.

Meatball Subs

Meatballs are a family favorite around here, and this is an easy way to make them a meal. Homemade meatballs inside warm buns with melted Gruyere on top...they'll be a huge hit!

INGREDIENTS

1½ pounds ground beef

1 onion, grated (I just use my cheese grater or you can finely chop)

2 tablespoons Italian seasoning blend

2 eggs

1 cup breadcrumbs

Salt and pepper

1 (8 ounce) can tomato sauce

1 cup shredded Gruyere cheese

Basil to garnish

4 large hoagie rolls

Preheat oven to 425 degrees. Line a baking sheet with foil and then lightly spray with cooking spray. Set aside.

In a large mixing bowl, combine the ground beef, grated onion, Italian seasoning, eggs, breadcrumbs, and a pinch of both salt and pepper. Combine mixture and then roll out into about 12 golf-ball-sized meatballs.

Place meatballs on prepared baking sheet and roast about 15 minutes in the oven. Meanwhile, split rolls down the middle.

When meatballs are cooked through, remove the baking sheet from the oven and assemble subs. Place three meatballs in each sub and drizzle tomato sauce over top (dividing it between each sub). Top subs with shredded Gruyere and some torn basil leaves. Place the subs back on your cookie sheet and pop it back in the oven for another five minutes or until the cheese is nice and melted.

Remove subs from oven and serve immediately.

BBQ Joes

You know how I love a sloppy joe! To me, they're just family food. This is your basic, eat-dinner-with-the-ones-you-love-on-a-weeknight kind of supper—and I love it! These joes come together in minutes and are delicious.

INGREDIENTS

Splash of extra virgin olive oil

1 pound ground beef

Salt and pepper

1 (14 ounce) can diced tomatoes, drained

1½ cups BBQ sauce

2 pieces frozen Texas toast per person, toasted in the oven per package directions

1½ cups Cheddar cheese, shredded

Pickled jalapeños to garnish (optional)

In a large skillet over medium-high heat, brown the ground beef in a splash of olive oil. Once the ground beef is browned, sprinkle in a little salt and pepper, reduce the heat to low, and stir in the tomatoes and BBQ sauce. Simmer uncovered for about 8 to 10 minutes.

Spoon the sloppy joe mixture over the top of the Texas toast. Sprinkle a little cheese on top and garnish with jalapeños.

Orange Marmalade Chicken Sandwiches

Just wait until you see how simple these sandwiches are to make! I love that the chicken cooks all day in my slow cooker and is ready and waiting for us after a busy day. This recipe is so simple and yet so full of flavor!

INGREDIENTS

1 to 1½ pounds boneless, skinless chicken breasts (frozen or thawed)

1 cup orange marmalade

1½ cups BBQ sauce

Burger buns

Chopped green onions to garnish (optional)

Orange zest to garnish (optional)

In a slow cooker, layer the chicken, marmalade, and BBQ sauce. Stir the marmalade and BBQ sauce together and make sure it's all over the chicken inside the slow cooker. Cover and cook on low for 7 to 8 hours or on high for 3 to 4 hours.

When you're ready to serve, remove the lid and shred the chicken right inside the slow cooker with two forks. Top the burger buns with the chicken mixture and garnish with green onions and/or orange zest.

Cumin Crusted Chicken

I can whip up Cumin Crusted Chicken in less than 30 minutes—with very little effort! I think the recipe is tasty with chicken breasts, but if pork cutlets rock your world, feel free to substitute. Some people are scared of cumin, but it's not hot and spicy at all! It just gives everything a nice smoked flavor and complements the cheese and other Mexican flavors.

INGREDIENTS

1 cup cornmeal

1 tablespoon ground cumin

Pinch of salt and pepper

1 egg, slightly beaten

4 boneless, skinless chicken breasts

1 cup Cheddar cheese, shredded

1½ cups salsa

Preheat the oven to 400 degrees.

In a large bowl, combine the cornmeal, cumin, and salt and pepper with a fork. In a second bowl, beat the egg.

Dredge each chicken breast in the cornmeal, then dredge it in egg, and then finally dredge it back in the cornmeal a second time, making sure to coat both sides.

Lay each chicken breast on a foil-lined baking sheet coated with cooking spray for easy cleanup. Bake the chicken for 20 minutes. Sprinkle cheese on the top of each chicken breast, then pop the baking sheet back into the oven for another 5 minutes or until the cheese is nice and bubbly.

Remove chicken from the oven and spoon salsa over the tops.

Chipotle and Corn Chicken Waffles

This isn't just a meal. It's a feast! It's simple, fun, and full of flavor. For an easy side dish, I like to roast cherry tomatoes in the oven at 425 degrees with a drizzle of olive oil and salt and pepper. Roast about 15 minutes. Summer has never tasted so delicious!

INGREDIENTS

4 boneless, skinless chicken breasts

1 (7 ounce) can chipotles in adobo sauce

1 cup orange juice

1 (at least 15 ounce) bottle BBQ sauce

1 box cornbread muffin mix (with ingredients to prepare per package)

1 red bell pepper, chopped

5 to 6 green onions, chopped

½ cup Monterey Jack cheese, shredded

½ cup corn kernels (frozen or fresh)

A few handfuls fresh spinach leaves

1 pint cherry tomatoes (optional)

Orange slices (optional)

At least 30 minutes before you're ready to grill (up to 24 hours), marinate the chicken in a giant plastic zip bag with 3 to 4 chipotles, a few spoonfuls of the adobo sauce, the orange juice, and 1 cup BBQ sauce. Refrigerate while marinating.

When you're ready to start grilling, remove the chicken breasts from marinade and discard the marinade. Grill the chicken over medium-high heat for about 7 minutes on each side or until the juices run clear and the chicken is fully cooked.

While the chicken is grilling, heat up a waffle iron. Spray the hot waffle iron with nonstick cooking spray.

In a small bowl, prepare the cornbread mix per package directions for basic cornbread muffins. Into the batter, stir the chopped bell pepper, green onions, cheese, and corn kernels (you can stir them in frozen). Pour the batter into the waffle iron and cook until golden.

Once the chicken is off the grill, add a few spinach leaves to the top of each cooked waffle and then top each waffle with sliced grilled chicken. Finish by drizzling a bit more BBQ sauce over the top.

Serve with cherry tomatoes and/or orange slices (optional).

Green Chile Chicken Baked Tacos

Taco night happens often at the Shull house. One night I decided to make yummy chicken tacos with whole green onions inside and crunchy bell pepper running through them. This is so fast that dinner was on the table in no time flat. This recipe is so simple to make and yummy to eat.

INGREDIENTS

1 pound cooked chicken, shredded

2 (4 ounce) jars of chopped green chilies

1 green bell pepper, chopped

1 cup sour cream

1 cup Pepper Jack or Monterey Jack cheese, shredded and divided

Salt and pepper

12 green onions (kept whole)

6 taco shells (I like the stand and stuff version for baking)

Salsa for garnishing, optional

Preheat the oven to 400 degrees.

Grease an 8 x 8 baking dish. Set aside.

In a large mixing bowl, combine the chicken, green chilies, bell pepper, sour cream, 1/2 cup shredded cheese, and a pinch of salt and pepper. Set aside.

Place two green onions against the bottom of each taco shell. Then fill each shell with some chicken mixture and stand the shell up in the prepared baking dish. Once all the shells are in the dish, sprinkle the remaining cheese over the tops. Bake for about 15 minutes or until the cheese is slightly browned and bubbly.

Remove the tacos from the oven and serve with a little salsa.

Pesto Quinoa and Chicken Stuffed Bell Peppers

Stuffed bell peppers look so fancy, but they are just so simple! I've made several varieties, and I can't seem to stop mixing and matching. It's full of veggies your family will love too.

INGREDIENTS

2 large bell peppers, any color

Drizzle of extra virgin olive oil

1 pound cooked chicken, shredded

1 box frozen spinach, thawed and drained of excess water

1 cup store-bought pesto (any variety; I use basil pesto)

1 cup cooked quinoa

2 cups mozzarella cheese, shredded and divided

Pinch of salt and pepper

Preheat the oven to 425 degrees.

Slice each bell pepper in half, length-wise. Remove the stem and seeds. Place all four halves in an 8 x 8 baking dish. Drizzle olive oil over the peppers and bake for about 10 minutes.

While the peppers are baking, combine the cooked chicken, spinach, pesto, quinoa, and 1 cup mozzarella cheese in a bowl with a good pinch of salt and pepper.

Remove the peppers from the oven and stuff them with chicken mixture (keep the peppers in the baking dish). Sprinkle the remaining cheese over all 4 peppers, then pop them back into the oven and bake another 15 minutes.

Remove from the oven and serve.

Peanut Pasta

I love peanut butter wrapped around chicken and pasta, with some soy sauce and sesame oil too—the perfect pasta supper, in my opinion! It's so comforting and delish without being too heavy.

INGREDIENTS

1 tablespoon extra virgin olive oil

2 tablespoons sesame oil

1 pound boneless, skinless chicken breasts, chopped to bite-sized pieces

Salt and pepper

10 to 12 green onions, chopped and divided

2 cloves garlic, chopped

4 tablespoons soy sauce

1 cup chicken stock

$\frac{1}{2}$ cup creamy peanut butter

1 pound angel hair pasta

Roasted peanuts to garnish

Bring a large pot of water to a boil for the pasta.

In a large skillet over medium-high heat, drizzle 1 tablespoon of olive oil and the sesame oil. Add the chicken to the skillet and cook them through, turning each piece over after about 4 minutes. Sprinkle a pinch of salt and pepper on top.

Add most of the chopped green onions (reserve a few to garnish), plus the garlic and soy sauce. Sauté for about two minutes. Then stir in the chicken stock, deglaze the pan (scrape up the little bits off the bottom), reduce heat to low, and stir in the peanut butter with a pinch more salt and pepper. Simmer for 5 to 8 minutes.

At this time, drop the pasta into the boiling water and cook to al dente (6 to 7 minutes). Drain off the water when the pasta is done and add the pasta to the chicken mixture. Toss to coat everything in the sauce. Serve each dish with a garnish of peanuts and a few extra green onions.

Sausage Tortellini Bake

This is always the recipe I take to people when they need a meal. Simple to assemble, hearty, delicious and great for freezing and reheating. All you do is layer everything together and bake. Done!

INGREDIENTS

1 pound breakfast sausage

2 (9 ounce) packages of refrigerated cheese tortellini

4 cups fresh or frozen broccoli florets

1 (15 ounce) jar of Alfredo sauce

1 cup milk

1 cup grated Parmesan cheese, plus a little extra for garnish

Extra virgin olive oil

Preheat oven to 400 degrees. Grease a 9 x 13 baking dish. Set aside.

In a skillet over medium-high heat, brown sausage in just a bit of olive oil. Once browned and crumbly, remove from heat and spread across prepared baking dish. Next, sprinkle over both packages of tortellini (uncooked!). After that, sprinkle broccoli florets over everything. Next, pour Alfredo sauce and milk over casserole. Take a large wooden spoon and lightly toss everything right inside your baking dish. Sprinkle your cheese over top.

Cover your baking dish with foil and bake about 20 minutes. Uncover and pop back into the oven to continue baking another 10 to 15 minutes or until everything is nice and bubbly.

Remove from oven and serve immediately with a little extra cheese on top.

Blueberry Banana Bread

I just love making quick breads (breads that don't require yeast). They're easy, they're moist, they're fast, and they're always yummy.

INGREDIENTS

1 stick of butter, melted and cooled

1/3 cup sugar

1/3 cup light brown sugar

2 eggs

5 ripe bananas, coarsely mashed

1/2 cup sweetened condensed milk

2 cups all-purpose flour

1 teaspoon salt

2 teaspoons baking powder

1 1/2 cups blueberries

Preheat oven to 350 degrees. Spray one standard loaf pan. Cream butter, 2 of the bananas and sugar in a large bowl using an electric mixer. Mix in eggs. Then mix in the remaining 3 bananas and sweetened condensed milk. Do not over-mix the batter. In a separate bowl, combine the flour, salt, and baking powder with a fork or whisk. Fold the banana mixture into the bowl with your dry ingredients. Do not over-mix! Stir in your blueberries.

Pour batter into your prepared pan. Bake 55 to 60 minutes or until a toothpick inserted in the middle comes out clean. Remove pan from oven and let bread rest in the pan about 45 minutes. After that, flip bread out onto a serving plate.

Slice bread and enjoy.

Nutella Cinnamon Rolls

We are big fans of Nutella in our house—it just goes with everything. This quick and easy recipe is perfect for not only weekend breakfasts but quick little weekday breakfasts too!

INGREDIENTS

1 can crescent rolls (I use the seamless sheets but the original kind works well too)

1 tablespoon butter, melted

1 cup Nutella

2 teaspoons cinnamon

2 or 3 splashes of milk

1 or 2 tablespoons powdered sugar

Preheat oven to 400 degrees. Line a baking sheet with foil and lightly spray with cooking spray for easy cleanup. Set aside.

Unroll crescent roll sheet (if you have the original kind with the perforated triangles, then just line them up in one big sheet and press the edges down). You should have a rectangle of dough.

Spread melted butter across the entire sheet of dough and then spread Nutella across (it doesn't have to reach the edges, just keep it mostly in the middle). Sprinkle cinnamon across the Nutella.

Roll up the dough into a log (so roll it up with the longer end). Slice the log into 6 or 8 pieces and lay each piece out on baking sheet. Bake 10 to 12 minutes or until lightly browned.

While cinnamon rolls are baking, make glaze. In a small bowl, mix milk and powdered sugar together with a fork. Add more milk if it's too thick and more sugar if it's too thin.

Remove cinnamon rolls from oven and immediately serve them with a drizzle of glaze.

Piña Colada Pie

I love making ice cream pies during the summer. They're cool, refreshing, great to make ahead for parties, and they're so simple that my kids can practically make them by themselves. Win, win, win. This ice cream pie has coconut gelato (or you can use ice cream or sherbet), whipped topping, pineapple chunks, and shredded coconut inside a graham cracker crust.

INGREDIENTS

1 graham cracker crust

1 pint coconut gelato, sherbet, or ice cream (thawed just enough to easily scoop out)

2 cups Cool Whip, thawed

1 (8 ounce) can crushed pineapple, drained

3 cups sweetened and flaked coconut, divided

In a mixing bowl, combine gelato, Cool Whip, pineapple, and 1½ cups of the coconut. Mix together with a wooden spoon until just combined. Spread this mixture into your prepared pie crust. Cover and freeze at least 2 hours (up to 2 days)!

When you're ready to serve, garnish the pie with toasted coconut. (I typically make a batch earlier in the day and just keep it in a baggie in the pantry until it's time to garnish.) Add the remaining 1½ cups of coconut to a clean, dry skillet over medium-high heat and toast up. It only takes about 4 minutes.

Garnish pie and serve frozen.

Snickerdoodle Bars

The other day at the pool, my girlfriend asked me for a bar recipe that wasn't a brownie...something kind of like a snickerdoodle. I immediately said she should take my original Neiman Marcus bar recipe, change out the cake mix, and add cinnamon for the perfect snickerdoodle bar. I tried it myself...and I think you'll love the results!

INGREDIENTS

1 box white cake mix

4 eggs

1 stick melted butter

4 tablespoons cinnamon, divided

1 box powdered sugar (about 4 cups)

1 (8 ounce) package cream cheese, softened

Preheat oven to 350 degrees. Grease one 9 x 13 pan.

In a bowl, combine cake mix, 2 eggs, melted butter, and 2 tablespoons cinnamon. Spread in bottom of pan. In a second bowl, beat with electric mixer powdered sugar, 2 more eggs, cream cheese, and remaining 2 tablespoons of cinnamon until smooth. Spread on top of crust mixture.

Bake 35 to 40 minutes until edges are brown and center set (it will still be slightly wobbly in the middle). Cool on counter 30 minutes, then refrigerate 2 hours or up to 2 days.

PB&J Bars

It's the beginning of the school year, and my mind always thinks of peanut butter and jelly—the quintessential lunch staple that is filling millions of lunch boxes each day. You'll feel like a kid again with this recipe.

INGREDIENTS

1 box of yellow cake mix

1/2 cup vegetable oil

2 eggs

1 cup creamy peanut butter

1 1/2 cups of your favorite jam
(I use strawberry)

Preheat oven to 350 degrees. Grease one 9 x 13 pan.

In a mixing bowl, combine cake mix, vegetable oil, and eggs with an electric mixer. Beat in peanut butter. Spread 2/3 of the mixture across the bottom of your pan.

Spread your jelly across the top of your base layer in your pan. Take the remaining 1/3 of your peanut butter batter and dot it across the top. It won't spread evenly across the top, so don't worry! Just drop it around and when it bakes, it will spread out.

Bake about 30 minutes or until the bars are brown around the edges. Let the bars cool on the counter at least 30 minutes before slicing and serving.

Bananas Foster Trifle

Andrew's favorite dessert is Bananas Foster, so I'm always looking for different spins on that classic recipe. So I thought, well, if he loves Banana Pudding and he loves Bananas Foster, he would love a hybrid. And thus, a recipe was born. This recipe serves 10 to 12. You can serve them individually (as pictured here) or out of one large trifle dish.

INGREDIENTS

1 prepared pound cake (you can make one or buy one, either way!)

1 (3.4 ounce) instant vanilla pudding mix

1 teaspoon rum extract

2 cups milk

1 (16 ounce) container Cool Whip, thawed

3 bananas, sliced

1 (12 ounce) jar caramel topping

1 1/2 cups toasted pecan pieces

Slice your pound cake into big chunks. Set aside.

In a mixing bowl, whisk together your dry pudding mix, rum extract and milk for 2 minutes (and it will thicken up a bit). Set aside once it has reached pudding consistency.

In one large trifle bowl or individual dishes, layer chunks of pound cake, sliced banana, pudding mixture, a little Cool Whip, drizzles of caramel, and some pecan pieces and then repeat. End with Cool Whip on top. Drizzle just a little more caramel over and top with your remaining toasted pecans. Cover and refrigerate at least 4 hours or even overnight.

Remove from fridge and serve.

*Life starts all over again
when it gets crisp in the fall.*

F. SCOTT FITZGERALD,
THE GREAT GATSBY

SEPTEMBER

DINNER

Andrea's Pulled Pork

BBQ Apple
Chicken Sandwiches

Italian Brisket Sandwiches

Loaded Chili

Sausage and Broccoli
Cheese Soup

Mom's Jambalaya

Spicy Chicken and
Sausage Soup

Mac and Peas

Maple Crusted Chicken

Beef Enchiladas

BREAKFAST

Taco Quiche

Slow Cooker Maple and
Oatmeal Baked Apples

DESSERT

Banana Cupcakes with Peanut Butter
Cream Cheese Frosting

Sweet Potato Cupcakes with Maple
Cream Cheese Frosting

Nutella Whoopie Pies

Caramel Apple Bread Pudding

Butterscotch-Maple No-Bake Cookies

Cinnamon Spice Bars

Andrea's Pulled Pork

This is the world's best pulled pork. It requires only four ingredients, and you can leave them alone in the slow cooker until you're ready to eat. This recipe makes a huge batch, so you can even serve it two nights in a row or use the leftovers on top of baked potatoes, in quesadillas and tacos, or over scrambled eggs.

INGREDIENTS

1 pork shoulder (also called pork butt or pork roast), 3 to 5 pounds

1 large onion, chopped into big chunks

2 cans of cola, not diet (I have used both regular and cherry cola)

1 (12 to 18 ounce) bottle BBQ sauce

Chopped green onions to garnish (optional)

Buns (if you're making sandwiches)

Place the pork and onions inside a slow cooker. Pour the soda on top of everything, cover, and cook on **high** for at least 8 to 10 hours.

Remove the lid after 8 to 10 hours. The meat should be falling apart at the touch of your fork. Transfer all the meat into a bowl and drain the slow cooker of the onions and liquid. Put the meat back in the slow cooker and shred it up with two forks. Stir in as much BBQ sauce as you like. At this point, you can serve immediately or you can turn the slow cooker to the "keep warm" setting and let it stay warm up to 4 or 5 hours until you're ready to eat.

BBQ Apple Chicken Sandwiches

Apple, onions, and slow cookers are staples at our house in the fall, and this recipe is now a staple too. The chicken gets so tender and moist, and the apple juice adds a little sweetness without being too overpowering. If you want to use frozen chicken, just make sure you cook it in the slow cooker at least 8 hours on low, 4 on high.

INGREDIENTS

1 pound boneless, skinless chicken breasts, uncooked

2 cups apple juice (or apple cider)

1 (at least 16 ounce) bottle BBQ sauce

1 onion, sliced and sautéed (optional)

Your favorite kind of bread (I use a whole wheat loaf from our bakery)

In a slow cooker, add the chicken, apple juice or cider, and entire bottle of BBQ sauce. Cook on low for 6 to 8 hours or on high for 3 to 4 hours. When you're ready to eat, put the chicken and some sauce from the slow cooker into a bowl and shred with two forks. Also add a little more sauce if needed.

Serve the shredded chicken with sautéed onions (optional) on top of your favorite bread.

Italian Brisket Sandwiches

I'm always trying to think of new ways to mix and match with brisket. It's such an easy cut of meat to cook in the slow cooker, so we eat it often, especially during fall and winter. This is an Italian style brisket and I serve it as an open-faced sandwich. So simple, right? My family eats it up, and I think yours will too!

INGREDIENTS

1 tablespoon extra virgin olive oil

1 brisket, 3 to 5 pounds

Salt and pepper

2 tablespoons Italian seasoning

1 onion, chopped

3 cloves garlic (leave whole, you'll remove them before serving)

1 (28 ounce) can whole tomatoes

1 cup beef stock, chicken stock, or water

1 (8 ounce) can tomato sauce

1 tablespoon brown sugar

1 tablespoon Worcestershire sauce

Burger buns

Parmesan cheese to garnish, grated

Basil to garnish

In a large pan over medium-high heat, brown both sides of the brisket in 1 tablespoon of olive oil (about 3 minutes on each side). Sprinkle salt and pepper liberally over each side. Once browned, put the brisket in a slow cooker. Sprinkle the Italian seasoning over the brisket and add the onion, whole pieces of garlic, tomatoes, and beef or chicken stock or water. Cover and cook on high for about 8 hours.

About 30 minutes to an hour before you're ready to eat, combine the tomato sauce, brown sugar, and Worcestershire sauce in a small bowl. Set aside.

Remove the brisket from the slow cooker and put it on a cutting board, then drain everything out of the slow cooker. Return the brisket to the hot slow cooker and shred it with two forks. Pour the tomato sauce mixture over everything, cover, and continue cooking for another 30 minutes to an hour.

When you're ready to serve, top each bun with some of the shredded brisket, a sprinkle of Parmesan, and some basil.

Loaded Chili

I didn't know what to call this bowl of goodness. I mean, it's kind of like a chili. It's kind of like veggie soup. But really it's just a bowl full of everything yummy. You can make it on the stove or in your slow cooker. Either way, this dish is so easy—and full of veggies! It will keep you going on busy weeknights. Enjoy!

INGREDIENTS

1 pound ground beef

Splash of extra virgin olive oil

1 onion, chopped

Salt and pepper

2 potatoes, chopped (I don't peel mine, but you can)

1 (28 ounce) can tomatoes

1 (15 ounce) can ranch style beans

1 (14 ounce) can green beans, drained

1 (1.35 ounce) packet onion soup mix

1 (.87 ounce) packet brown gravy mix

1 (1 ounce) packet ranch salad dressing mix

1 box frozen spinach, thawed and drained of excess water

1 cup frozen corn

In a large Dutch oven (that's a big pot!) over medium-high heat, brown the ground beef in a splash of olive oil. Add the onion and some salt and pepper and sauté for a few minutes. Add the potatoes, tomatoes, beans, green beans, and all three packets of seasoning. Bring the mixture to a boil, then reduce the heat, cover, and simmer for about 30 minutes or until the potatoes are tender. Once the potatoes are about done, add the spinach and corn, cover, and cook for an additional 5 minutes.

Ladle into bowls and serve.

Sausage and Broccoli Cheese Soup

This soup is just delicious. Delicious. I wanted to make a broccoli cheese soup but I also wanted to add a protein to give it a little more substance. So I added an Italian-style chicken sausage. Perfect for chilly nights. Perfect for busy families. Perfect for warming up.

INGREDIENTS

1 pound Italian-style sausage (I use chicken sausage but you can use pork or turkey)

2 tablespoons extra virgin olive oil

1 onion, chopped

Salt and pepper

1 tablespoon all-purpose flour

3 cups milk

4 cups chopped broccoli (fresh or frozen brought to room temp)

2 cups Cheddar cheese, shredded

In a large pot over medium-high heat, brown the sausage in about 2 tablespoons olive oil. Once it's browned and crumbly, add the onion along with a pinch of salt and pepper and sauté for 3 or 4 minutes.

Sprinkle in the flour and then immediately whisk in the milk and continue to whisk about a minute. Reduce the heat to low and stir in the broccoli. Add a pinch more salt and pepper and continue to simmer over low heat, stirring frequently for 15 to 20 minutes. Stir in the cheese and stir until it's all combined and melted.

Ladle into bowls and serve.

Mom's Jambalaya

I'm not Cajun, but I love me some jambalaya! My mama adds chicken, sausage, and shrimp, but you can mix and match. I prefer a nice smoky pork sausage, but any sausage you use is fine. Note my instructions for cooking the rice for this dish. Bonus tip: You can use a store-bought jambalaya mix instead of your own rice and seasoning and make this dish on top of the stove.

INGREDIENTS

1 pound boneless, skinless chicken breasts, uncooked and cut into pieces

8 ounce sausage links, cut into 1-inch pieces

1 (14 ounce) can diced tomatoes

1 (14 ounce) can Rotel tomatoes

2 (10 ounce) cans chicken broth

1 tablespoon Cajun seasoning

1 teaspoon cumin

1½ cups long grain rice, uncooked

2 handfuls frozen shrimp

In a slow cooker, layer the chicken, sausage, tomatoes, Rotel tomatoes, chicken broth, and both kinds of seasoning. Cook on low for 6 to 8 hours or on high for 3 to 4 hours. If you're using a standard, not fast-cooking long grain rice, then 1 hour before you're ready to eat, add the rice and cover. If you're using a quick-cooking rice, then add about 20 minutes before you're ready to eat. Add the shrimp the last 10 minutes before you're ready to eat.

Spicy Chicken and Sausage Soup

This soup provides lots of flavor, lots of veggies—and requires little time on your part. You just throw your ingredients in and the slow cooker does all the work for this one-pot meal! I use a sweet Italian chicken sausage, and if you're not serving little ones, you should try a spicy sausage for a real kick! But you can substitute a turkey sausage or pork sausage if that's best for you.

INGREDIENTS

1 pound boneless, skinless chicken breasts, uncooked (not frozen)

½ pound sausage, cut into bite-sized pieces (precooked or uncooked)

1 green or red bell pepper, chopped

1 tablespoon chili powder

1 (14 ounce) can Rotel tomatoes

2 cups chicken broth

Big pinch salt and pepper

1 box frozen spinach, thawed and drained of excess water

½ pound uncooked pasta (I use shells)

Chopped green onions (optional)

In a slow cooker, combine the chicken, sausage, bell pepper, chili powder, tomatoes, and chicken broth. Add a big pinch of salt and pepper. Stir and cover. Cook on low for 6 to 7 hours or on high for 3 to 4 hours.

About 30 minutes before you're ready to serve, shred the chicken breasts right inside the slow cooker with two forks. Then stir in the spinach and uncooked pasta. Return the lid, move the heat to high, and cook for an additional 30 minutes or until the pasta is tender.

Ladle the soup into bowls and garnish with chopped green onions.

Mac and Peas

If I can get my kids to eat peas, I really don't care that it's wrapped around creamy mac and cheese. A hearty side or a vegetarian main dish...No matter which, it's easy peasy!

INGREDIENTS

1 pound elbow pasta

3 tablespoons extra virgin olive oil

1 shallot, chopped

3 tablespoons flour

2 cups milk

2 cups shredded sharp white Cheddar cheese

2 cups frozen peas

Bring a large pot of water up to a boil and then drop in pasta. Cook about 6 to 8 minutes or until pasta is al dente. Drain and reserve.

While pasta is cooking, add olive oil to a second pot along with your shallot and sauté about 4 to 5 minutes. Next, whisk in flour and cook another minute. Then whisk in milk. Let sauce thicken together over medium heat about 10 minutes or until sauce is thick and bubbly. Whisk in cheese and then once it's melted, stir in your frozen peas and cook about two minutes. Stir in one big pinch of salt and pepper at the end.

Toss reserved pasta with sauce, serve immediately, and enjoy!

Maple Crusted Chicken

One of the best flavors of fall is maple syrup. I am quite the syrup snob; once I tasted real maple syrup (not regular old pancake syrup), I couldn't go back. And Bisquick plus syrup plus chicken equals FANTASTIC! It's not too sweet (so don't be scared). It's just really, really good. You're going to love this dinner. It's quick, it's easy, it's fall.

INGREDIENTS

¾ cup Bisquick

½ tablespoon black pepper

1 egg

1 pound boneless, skinless chicken breasts, uncooked

4 tablespoons maple syrup (plus a little more to drizzle at the end)

2 tablespoons butter, melted

Preheat the oven to 400 degrees.

In one shallow dish (I use a pie plate), combine Bisquick and pepper. In a second shallow dish, beat the egg. Pour 1 tablespoon of syrup on each chicken breast, coating both sides. Then dip it first in the Bisquick, coating well, then in the egg mix, coating both sides. Then dip it one more time in the Bisquick.

Place the chicken on a foil-lined cookie sheet sprayed with cooking spray for easy cleanup. Brush half of the melted butter over the tops of the chicken and bake for 8 minutes. Flip the chicken over and brush the remaining half of the melted butter on the opposite side and finish cooking for another 8 minutes. The chicken should be brown and kind of crispy with the juices running clear when pierced with a fork.

Serve each chicken breast with a drizzle of syrup.

Beef Enchiladas

I don't have time on a busy weeknight to make fancy enchiladas, but I do have time to make my simple Beef Enchiladas! They're on the table in less than 30 minutes. To make them in advance, keep them in the fridge until time to bake them, but add a few minutes to the baking time. If you freeze them, do so without the sauce on top and bring them to room temp before baking.

INGREDIENTS

1 pound ground beef (or ground turkey)

2 tablespoons chili powder or (1 ounce) packet taco seasoning

1 (10 ounce) can Cheddar cheese soup

1 (14 ounce) can Rotel tomatoes

1 (4 ounce) can chopped green chilies

8 tortillas (flour or whole wheat work best)

1 (16 ounce) bottle enchilada sauce

Chopped green onions to garnish

Preheat oven to 400 degrees.

In a large skillet over medium-high heat, brown the ground beef until it's nice and crumbly. Stir in the chili powder, soup, tomatoes, and green chilies (don't drain any of it). Reduce the heat to low and simmer for 2 to 3 minutes. While the mixture is simmering, spray an 8 x 8 baking dish with cooking spray. Set aside.

Fill each tortilla with ground beef mixture. Roll them over and lay them seam side down in the baking dish. Pour the enchilada sauce over all the enchiladas once they're in the baking dish. Bake them for about 8 or 10 minutes or until they're nice and bubbly.

Remove the enchiladas from oven and serve with green onions on top.

Taco Quiche

The taco meat really gives this quiche a punch. Don't worry about the jalapeños and Pepper Jack being too spicy—it really isn't. The jalapeños mellow out quite a bit during the cooking process and the cheese has just the right amount of bite to it.

INGREDIENTS

1 pound ground beef

1 packet taco seasoning

1 onion, chopped

2 jalapeños, chopped

4 eggs, beaten

1½ cups milk

1 can chopped green chilies

2 cups Pepper Jack cheese, shredded

green onions to garnish

1 refrigerated pie crust, brought to room temperature

Preheat oven to 350 degrees. Fit a pie plate with one sheet of your pie crust. Set aside.

Brown your ground beef over medium high heat. Once brown, sprinkle in your taco seasoning and add in your onions and jalapeños and brown another 5 to 6 minutes. Remove from heat and set aside.

In a medium bowl, combine eggs, milk, chilies, and cheese. Fold in ground beef mixture. Pour mixture into unbaked pie shell and bake about 45 minutes. Remove from oven and let stand 10 minutes before slicing into wedges.

I always set my quiche on top of a baking sheet in the oven in case there is any bubbling over. This makes for easy cleanup.

Slow Cooker Maple and Oatmeal Baked Apples

September is the month where apples shine. I love to kick off our September with some yummy baked apples in my slow cooker. Not only is this method simple but it's delicious too. This could be a snack, a breakfast, or even a dessert. Let apples shine in your kitchen this month!

INGREDIENTS

4 to 6 firm apples (I use Gala, but you could also use Jonagold, Rome, or Golden Delicious)

2 cups oatmeal (not quick cooking)

2 tablespoons cinnamon

½ cup brown sugar

Maple syrup for drizzling

1 tablespoon butter per apple

Core each apple, creating a nice place to put your oatmeal mixture.

In a small bowl, combine oatmeal, cinnamon, and brown sugar with a spoon. Stuff each apple with oatmeal mixture and place them inside slow cooker. (I use a slow cooker liner for easy cleanup!)

Drizzle maple syrup over the tops of each apple and then place one tablespoon of butter on top of each one. Close the lid of your slow cooker and cook on low 2½ to 3 hours. Remove and serve.

Banana Cupcakes with Peanut Butter Cream Cheese Frosting

The beginning of the school year just feels synonymous with pea-nut butter. These cupcakes are extra moist because of the mashed bananas inside, but what really takes the cake is the frosting.

INGREDIENTS

1 cup all-purpose flour

½ cup sugar

1 teaspoon baking soda

1 tablespoon pumpkin pie spice

½ cup vegetable oil

2 eggs

2 cups mashed bananas
(3 or 4 bananas)

1 (8 ounce) package cream cheese, softened

3 cups powdered sugar

1 cup creamy peanut butter

1 tablespoon milk

Preheat oven to 350 degrees.

Place 12 cupcake liners into one (12-count) muffin tin. Set aside.

In a large mixing bowl, combine flour, sugar, baking soda, and pumpkin pie spice with a whisk. Set aside. In a second mixing bowl, beat with an electric mixer the vegetable oil, eggs and bananas. Slowly pour the banana mixture into flour mixture and beat until just blended (do not over-beat the batter).

Divide batter among 12 cupcake liners and bake 16 to 18 minutes or until a toothpick inserted in the middle comes out clean. Remove from oven and let cool 5 minutes in the pan before removing and continuing to cool on a wire rack.

Allow cupcakes to completely cool before frosting.

To make frosting, beat cream cheese, powdered sugar, peanut butter, and milk together with an electric mixer. Add more sugar if the frosting is too thin and more milk if it's too thick. Once frosting reaches desired consistency, frost each cupcake with a dollop. Refrigerate until ready to serve.

Sweet Potato Cupcakes with Maple Cream Cheese Frosting

If you're a girl after my own heart, you will totally justify this indulgence by reminding yourself that there is a vegetable inside. One cupcake with a vegetable inside is healthy, right? Even if it does have a little frosting on top!

INGREDIENTS

1 box spice cake mix

2 (3.4 ounce) boxes instant vanilla pudding

½ cup vegetable oil

1¼ cups water

4 eggs

1 cup canned sweet potato, drained and lightly mashed with a fork

1 (8 ounce) package cream cheese, at room temperature

3 cups powdered sugar

¼ cup pure maple syrup

Ground cinnamon to garnish

Preheat oven to 350 degrees. Line 2 (12 count each) muffin tins with cupcake liners. Set aside.

In mixing bowl, combine cake mix, puddings, oil, water, and eggs with electric mixer. Add in sweet potatoes and mix until blended. Pour into prepared cupcake liners until they are each about ⅔ full.

Bake 18 to 20 minutes or until toothpick inserted in the center comes out clean.

Let cupcakes rest on the counter in the pans 10 minutes. Then remove the cupcakes onto a cooling rack to finish cooling.

To make the frosting, beat your cream cheese, powdered sugar, and maple syrup in a mixing bowl until combined. Add more powdered sugar if your frosting is too thin and more maple syrup if it's too thick.

Frost cooled cupcakes with maple cream cheese frosting and garnish with a little ground cinnamon.

Store cupcakes in the fridge until ready to serve.

Nutella Whoopie Pies

If you're a Nutella person, this will be your kind of whoopie pie. I added some toffee pieces to them for a little crunch (and because I just love a little toffee). You could go crazy and use butterscotch chips instead, or chocolate chips, or dried cranberries, or chopped pecans. Make these your own.

INGREDIENTS

1 box chocolate cake mix

½ cup vegetable oil

2 eggs

¼ cup water

1 (13 ounce) jar Nutella

1 to 2 cups toffee pieces

Preheat oven to 350 degrees. Combine cake mix, oil, eggs, and water in bowl.

Drop by 2 tablespoons onto lined cookie sheet (leave about an inch between each cookie) and bake 9 to 10 minutes. Cool on pan 5 minutes, move to wire rack and cool 15 more minutes.

Take one cookie and place a tablespoon or so of Nutella in the center. Sprinkle a little toffee over the top of the Nutella. Press another cookie on top (this will spread the Nutella out to the edge). Holding your whoopie pie, sprinkle your toffee over the sides so that a little crunch sticks to the sides of your whoopie pie.

Caramel Apple Bread Pudding

I love bread pudding! If you've never made one before, you should. They're warm and cozy and perfect for chilly nights. Served alone, with a dollop of whipped cream or a scoop of ice cream, you can't go wrong. This is cozy comfort food.

INGREDIENTS

1 loaf of Challah (or Brioche) bread torn into pieces

4 cups milk

3 eggs, lightly beaten

1 cup grated apples (I use 2 Granny Smiths and grate them with my cheese grater)

1 cup sugar

1 cup brown sugar

1 tablespoon cinnamon

1 cup pecan pieces

1 (12 ounce) jar caramel topping, divided

Preheat oven to 350 degrees. Grease a 9 x 13 baking dish. Set aside.

Tear your loaf of bread into bite sized pieces and place them in baking dish. Pour milk over bread and let it stand about 10 minutes. Stir eggs together with the grated apple, sugar, brown sugar, cinnamon, pecan pieces and 1/2 cup caramel topping. Pour this mixture over bread mixture.

Bake uncovered for 40 to 45 minutes. Remove from oven and immediately serve. I cut mine into portions and then drizzled additional caramel topping over each piece. If you're serving this in a mason jar or trifle dish, drizzle caramel between the layers of bread pudding.

Butterscotch-Maple No-Bake Cookies

My kids love making no bake cookies, and I love it because they're just so simple. Maple syrup plus peanut butter plus butterscotch equals one delicious cookie! There is something so special about making cookies with your kiddos. And the best part about these cookies? You don't have to wait for them to come out of the oven!

INGREDIENTS

2 cups sugar

1 stick butter

½ cup milk

1 cup peanut butter

2 tablespoons maple syrup

3 cups oatmeal

1 cup butterscotch chips

Wax paper for cooling

In a heavy saucepan over medium-high heat, bring sugar, butter, and milk to a boil. Boil about a minute, then stir in peanut butter, syrup, and oatmeal. Remove from heat and fold in your chips.

Drop by the tablespoon full onto wax paper to finish cooling (and they'll harden up). Once cooled, store in an airtight container.

Cinnamon Spice Bars

A little cinnamon, a little spice, and a whole lot of yumminess. This is one of those bar recipes that you should eat while drinking cocoa cuddled up in a blanket watching TV. The perfect bar for fall, or the holidays, or any old day.

INGREDIENTS

1 box of spice cake mix

4 eggs

1 stick melted butter

4 cups powdered sugar

1 (8 ounce) package of cream cheese, softened

1 tablespoon cinnamon

Preheat oven to 350 degrees. Grease a 9 x 13 baking dish.

In a bowl, combine cake mix, 2 eggs, and melted butter. Spread batter in bottom of pan.

In a second bowl, beat with electric mixer, powdered sugar, 2 more eggs, cream cheese, and cinnamon until smooth. Spread on top of crust mixture.

Bake 35 to 40 minutes until edges are brown and center set (it will still be slightly wobbly in the middle).

Cool on counter 30 minutes, then refrigerate 2 hours or up to 2 days.

I'm so glad I live in a world where there are Octobers.

~L. M. Montgomery,
Anne of Green Gables

OCTOBER

DINNER

Butternut Squash Soup

Spicy Sausage and
Potato Soup

Taco Chili

Taco Tortellini Soup

Tex-Mex Chicken and
Rice Soup

BBQ Pork Tacos

Brown Sugar Brisket

Beer Cheese Joes

Mexican Beef over Rice

Pumpkin Rigatoni

BREAKFAST

Pumpkin Waffles

Butterscotch Monkey Bread

DESSERT

Pumpkin Angel Food Cake

Candy Corn Cupcakes

Caramel Apple Cider Cupcakes

Chocolate Apple Pecan Cobbler

Peanut Butter S'mores Bars

Chocolate Chip Pumpkin Bars

Butternut Squash Soup

A mug of butternut squash soup? Don't you just get warm and cozy thinking about it? This soup will warm you up, heart and soul. You just roast the veggies, blend them up a bit, simmer them for a few minutes, and you're ready to go. The best part about this soup is how well it heats up for several days in a row.

INGREDIENTS

1 butternut squash, peeled and chopped into chunks

1 onion, chopped

3 apples (I use Braeburn), chopped into chunks

4 to 5 tablespoons extra virgin olive oil

Salt and pepper

4 cups chicken stock

1 teaspoon cinnamon

1 teaspoon nutmeg

1 teaspoon chili powder

2 to 3 splashes of milk or cream

Sour cream to garnish

Preheat the oven to 450 degrees.

On a foil-lined baking sheet, toss the squash, onion, and apple pieces with 4 to 5 tablespoons of olive oil and lots of salt and pepper. Roast for about 45 minutes in the oven.

Remove the baking sheet from oven and either put everything in a standard blender to blend or put everything in a big pot and use an immersion blender to blend. Add the chicken stock and blend. (I only blend mine a tad. I like the texture of a chunkier soup.) Once the mixture is blended, make sure everything is in a big pot on the stove. Add cinnamon, nutmeg, and chili powder. Bring the heat to medium-high and let it get bubbly, then simmer for about 10 minutes over low heat. Stir in the milk the last 2 to 3 minutes and simmer. Remove from heat.

Serve with a dollop of sour cream.

Spicy Sausage and Potato Soup

My favorite kind of soup is one that bubbles away all day in my slow cooker. For this recipe, I use spicy Italian sausage, but you can use a mild Italian instead if you're worried about it being too hot for anyone in your family. You can use pork, chicken, or turkey sausage...whatever your family enjoys.

INGREDIENTS

1 pound bulk Italian sausage

1 tablespoon extra virgin olive oil

2 russet potatoes, peeled and chopped into chunks

1 onion, chopped

1 (28 ounce) can whole peeled tomatoes

1 (10 ounce) can Rotel tomatoes

2 cups chicken stock

1 box frozen spinach, thawed and drained of excess water

Parmesan cheese to garnish, grated

In a large skillet over medium-high heat, brown the sausage in 1 tablespoon of olive oil. Once the sausage is browned and crumbly, place it in a slow cooker along with the next 5 ingredients (potatoes through chicken stock). Stir, cover, and cook on low for 7 to 8 hours or on high for 4 hours.

About 15 minutes before you're ready to serve, stir in the spinach. Cover and cook an additional 15 minutes or so. Ladle the soup into bowls and top with Parmesan cheese before serving.

Taco Chili

My husband has been calling this Taco Chili "the hybrid" for years. It's thick like a chili but with the flavors of a taco soup. It's a one-pot meal for a cold fall (or winter) day—perfection! And if you want, you can let this baby simmer away for hours, even transferring it to your slow cooker to cook on low for 6 hours or so. So simple and satisfying.

INGREDIENTS

1 pound ground beef

1 onion, chopped

1 packet ranch dressing mix

1 packet taco seasoning

1 (14 ounce) can Rotel tomatoes

1 (4 ounce) can chopped green chilies

1 (15 ounce) can ranch-style beans, undrained

1 (8 ounce) can tomato sauce

Chips, cheese, sour cream to garnish

In a large Dutch oven and over medium-high heat, brown the ground beef. Add the onion and sauté for 5 to 6 minutes. Add both seasoning packets and stir until they are combined with the meat and onion mixture. Add the tomatoes, chilies, beans, and tomato sauce. Reduce the heat to low and simmer at least 10 minutes.

Taco Tortellini Soup

During fall and winter, we eat some version of taco or tortilla soup at least once a week. It's easy, it's flavorful, and it's always a hit with my family. This version uses refrigerated cheese tortellini. Simple goodness in a bowl.

INGREDIENTS

1 pound ground beef

1 onion, chopped

1 (1 ounce) package of taco seasoning

1 (10 ounce) can Rotel tomatoes

2 cups of chicken stock

1 (15 ounce) can black beans, rinsed and drained

1 (8 ounce) can tomato sauce

1½ cups frozen corn

2 (9 ounce) packages of refrigerated cheese tortellini

Shredded Cheddar cheese to garnish

Salt and pepper

Extra virgin olive oil

In a skillet over medium-high heat, brown up your ground beef in a little drizzle of olive oil. Once it's brown and crumbly, add in a pinch of salt and pepper and then transfer the ground beef to your slow cooker.

Next, add in your chopped onion, taco seasoning, Rotel, stock, beans, and tomato sauce. Cover and cook on low 6 to 8 hours or on high 3 to 4 hours. About 30 minutes before you're ready to serve, remove the lid and add in your refrigerated tortellini and frozen corn. Cover and cook on high for the next 30 minutes.

After that, ladle into bowls, garnish with a little cheddar, and serve.

Tex-Mex Chicken and Rice Soup

In the fall and winter, we have soup for supper just about every other night. This is a delicious chicken and rice version with a Tex-Mex flair—and best of all, it's all done in the slow cooker!

INGREDIENTS

1 pound boneless, skinless chicken breasts, uncooked (frozen or thawed)

1 (10 ounce) can Rotel tomatoes

1 (1 ounce) packet taco seasoning mix

1 (10 ounce) can tomato soup

2 cups chicken stock

1 cup instant rice (I use brown), uncooked

1 cup Cheddar cheese, shredded

1 cup frozen corn or 1 (15 ounce) can corn, drained

Green onions to garnish, chopped

In a slow cooker, combine the chicken, tomatoes, taco seasoning, soup, and chicken stock. Cover and cook on low for 6 to 8 hours or high for 3 to 4 hours.

About 30 minutes before you're ready to eat, shred the chicken right inside the slow cooker with two forks. Stir in the rice, cheese, and corn. Turn the slow cooker to high heat, cover, and cook for another 30 minutes.

Ladle the soup into bowls and garnish with some chopped green onions.

BBQ Pork Tacos

The slow cooker is without a doubt my very favorite way to make pulled pork! Sometimes, instead of serving it on buns, we pile it into taco shells and top it with shredded cheese and green onions. This would be a great way to use your leftovers too. Make a big batch of pulled pork and serve it two different ways, two nights in a row.

INGREDIENTS

1 pork shoulder (also called pork butt or pork roast), 3 to 5 pounds

1 large onion, chopped into big chunks

2 cans cola, not diet (I have used both regular and cherry cola)

1 (12 to 18 ounce) bottle BBQ sauce

Taco shells

Green onions, chopped to garnish (optional)

Cheddar cheese, grated to garnish

Place the pork and onion inside a slow cooker. Pour the soda on top of everything, cover, and cook on **high** for at least 8 to 10 hours.

Remove the lid after 8 to 10 hours and the meat should be falling apart at the touch of your fork. Remove all the meat from the slow cooker and put it into a bowl, then drain the slow cooker of the onions and liquid. Add the meat back in the slow cooker and shred it with two forks. Stir in as much BBQ sauce as you like.

You can serve immediately or keep the pork warm for another hour or two in the slow cooker. When you're ready to eat, fill the taco shells with pork and top with a sprinkle of green onions (optional) and some Cheddar cheese.

Brown Sugar Brisket

This brisket recipe is particularly yummy because it has a brown sugar and mustard glaze, a tasty little addition to a tender brisket. I use apple juice because it adds great flavor to the meat, but if you prefer, you can use half apple juice and half water. My kiddos love brisket!

INGREDIENTS

1 flat-trimmed brisket, 3 to 5 pounds	1 tablespoon yellow mustard
Drizzle of extra virgin olive oil	1 onion, chopped
Sprinkles of salt and pepper	4 cups apple juice (or 2 cups apple juice and 2 cups water)
½ cup brown sugar	

In a large skillet over medium-high heat, brown each side of the brisket in a drizzle of olive oil (about 4 minutes each side). Sprinkle salt and pepper over each side.

While the brisket is browning, combine the brown sugar and mustard in a small bowl. Set aside.

Place the browned brisket in the slow cooker. Rub the brown sugar mix all over the brisket. Add the onion and pour the apple juice (or apple juice and water) on top. Cover and cook on high for about 8 hours.

When you're ready to eat, remove the brisket from the liquid (discard the liquid) and put it on a cutting board. Shred the brisket and serve.

Beer Cheese Joes

I love making beer cheese soup. But one day I thought, Hmm, that would make a good sloppy joe! So, I married the two, and voilà! A beer cheese joe! Dinner mixed and matched.

INGREDIENTS

1 pound ground beef	1 cup beer (I use a lager)
1 tablespoon extra virgin olive oil	1 cup Cheddar cheese, shredded
Generous pinches of salt and pepper	Burger buns
1 onion, chopped	Chives to garnish, chopped
1 tablespoon flour	

In a large skillet over medium-high heat, brown the ground beef in 1 tablespoon of olive oil. Once it's browned and crumbly, add the onion and a generous pinch of salt and pepper. Sauté for about 4 minutes. Sprinkle the flour over the meat and onion mixture, then slowly pour the beer in the pan. Reduce the heat to low and stir the beef and flour together until the mixture starts to thicken a bit (about 3 minutes). Add the cheese and stir until it's melted (about 3 minutes). Top each burger bun with a scoop of sloppy joe mixture and garnish with a few chives.

Mexican Beef over Rice

You can also serve this yummy beef mixture over tortillas, quinoa, or even macaroni noodles!

INGREDIENTS

1 pound ground beef

2 tablespoons chili powder

1 (4 ounce) can chopped green chilies

2 cups salsa

1 (15 ounce) can chili beans

10 green onions, chopped

1½ cups grated Cheddar (I use sharp white cheddar)

1 cup brown rice

2 cups water

Extra virgin olive oil

Salt and pepper

In a large skillet over medium-high heat, brown ground beef in just a drizzle of olive oil. Once browned and crumbly, add in a pinch of salt and pepper along with chili powder.

While beef is browning, add water and rice to a small pot, cover, and bring to a boil. Once it starts to boil, keep covered and reduce heat to low and allow the rice to cook according to package instructions.

Meanwhile, add the chopped green chilies, salsa, chili beans, and green onions to the ground beef mixture. Reduce heat to low and allow to simmer.

Once rice has absorbed all of the water and is cooked, fluff it up with a fork and divide out among plates. Top rice with a big scoop of ground beef mixture and top with shredded cheese and a few extra chopped green onions.

Pumpkin Rigatoni

If you've never had pumpkin in a savory dish before, you've been missing out. Pumpkin pairs perfectly with savory suppers—especially pasta suppers! Pumpkin, bacon, Parmesan... Hello, fall!

INGREDIENTS

1 pound rigatoni

12 slices bacon

2 garlic cloves, chopped

1 red onion, chopped

1 cup chicken stock

1 cup pumpkin (not pumpkin pie filling) cubed and cooked

3 tablespoons half and half, cream, or milk

Freshly grated Parmesan cheese

Handful of chopped basil

Extra virgin olive oil

Salt and pepper

Bring one large pot of water up to a boil for your pasta. Drop pasta in and cook 5 to 7 minutes until al dente.

In another large skillet, heat a tablespoon of olive oil over medium-high heat. Place bacon in pan and crisp up on both sides. Once crispy, remove bacon to a paper towel to drain. Add onion and garlic to your bacon drippings in the skillet and sauté 4 to 5 minutes. Once onion is sautéed, pour in chicken stock to deglaze your pan. Lower heat to low and let chicken stock simmer 2 to 3 minutes. Stir in pumpkin and heat through about 3 minutes.

Meanwhile, break bacon into bite-sized pieces. Set aside.

Drain pasta and add to pumpkin mixture. Stir in half and half and Parmesan. Finally, add back in crispy bacon pieces and basil.

Remove from skillet, ladle pasta into bowls and serve with a little more Parmesan and basil.

Pumpkin Waffles

To make these ahead of time, prepare as directed and put them in the freezer. When ready to heat, pop them in the microwave for about 45 seconds.

INGREDIENTS

2½ cups Bisquick

1 cup canned pumpkin

2 eggs, lightly beaten

1 cup milk

2 tablespoons vegetable oil

2 tablespoons pumpkin pie spice

Maple syrup to drizzle

Preheat your waffle iron.

In a large mixing bowl, combine the first 6 ingredients with a spoon. Do not over mix, just combine well.

When your waffle iron is hot, lightly spray it with a cooking spray. Add about ½ cup of batter at a time if you're making large waffles. Close lid and wait for waffle to reach your desired crispness.

Remove and serve immediately with a drizzle of maple syrup.

Butterscotch Monkey Bread

Breakfast can be such a special time of the day (especially on cool autumn mornings) and having people over for brunch on the weekend is probably my favorite way to entertain. However, no one wants to fuss with something complicated. And yet, you still want a show-stopper. Served with a cup of coffee or a big glass of milk, you and your family will flip over this little gem!

INGREDIENTS

½ cup sugar

½ teaspoon cinnamon

2 (16.3 ounce) cans refrigerated flaky layer biscuit dough, cut into quarters

¾ cup firmly packed brown sugar

½ cup butter

¼ cup light corn syrup

1 small box (3.4 ounce) instant butterscotch pudding mix

Preheat oven to 350 degrees. Spray a Bundt pan with cooking spray.

In a small bowl, combine sugar and cinnamon. Dredge biscuit quarters in sugar mixture to coat. Layer in prepared pan. (At this point, you could cover your pan and pop it in the fridge until the next morning.)

In a small saucepan, combine brown sugar, butter, corn syrup, and instant pudding mix. Cook over medium-high heat stirring constantly until mixture comes to a boil. Boil one minute. Pour over layered biscuits. Bake 40 minutes. Let pan sit 5 minutes before inverting it onto platter to serve.

Pumpkin Angel Food Cake

Three little ingredients plus a dollop of whipped cream. So simple, so yummy, so fall.

INGREDIENTS

1 box angel food cake mix, found with the cake mixes (select one that only requires you add water)

1 (15 ounce) can canned pumpkin

1½ tablespoons cinnamon

Whipped cream to garnish

Preheat oven to 350 degrees. Grease a 9 x 13 baking dish. Set aside.

In a mixing bowl, combine the box of angel food cake mix and pumpkin with an electric mixer. Once combined, beat in the cinnamon.

Pour batter into prepared baking dish and bake 25 to 30 minutes or until lightly browned on top and a toothpick inserted in the middle comes out clean.

Remove from oven, cut into squares, and dollop with a little whipped cream and a sprinkle of cinnamon.

Candy Corn Cupcakes

How cute are these? And the best part of all—they are super easy to make!

INGREDIENTS

1 box white cake mix

4 egg whites

1¼ cups water

½ cup vegetable oil

Yellow and orange food coloring

Cupcake liners

½ cup butter, softened

4 cups powdered sugar

3-4 tablespoons milk

1 teaspoon almond extract

White sprinkles, optional

Candy corn

Preheat oven to 350 degrees. Combine cake mix, egg whites, water, and vegetable oil. Divide batter into two bowls. Color one bowl yellow and the other orange.

Double line cupcake tin. (I always use two liners when baking cupcakes. This way, the outside liner stays cute and the design isn't lost when it's baked against the cupcake.) One recipe will make about 16 cupcakes.

Fill liners about halfway with yellow cake mix. Lightly bang the cupcake tin against the counter so that all of the yellow batter settles firmly in the tin. Top with orange batter. Bake 17 to 22 minutes or until toothpick inserted comes out clean. Let cool 5 minutes in tin before cooling completely on cooling rack (about 20 minutes).

To make the frosting, beat butter, sugar, and milk in a bowl. Add in almond extract. Top each cupcake with frosting and decorate with sprinkles and candy corn.

Caramel Apple Cider Cupcakes

The apple makes the cupcakes extra moist and delicious. To grate mine, I use a cheese grater and run my apple across it like you would a block of cheese. You could also substitute applesauce for the grated apple in this recipe.

INGREDIENTS

1 box spice cake mix

1 cup apple cider (plus a little more for your frosting)

3 eggs

⅓ cup vegetable oil

1 cup grated apple

1 cup caramel topping (the kind you would use for ice cream)

3 cups powdered sugar

1 stick butter, softened

Preheat your oven to 350 degrees.

Line 2 (12 count) muffin tins with cupcake liners.

In a mixing bowl, combine spice cake mix, cider, eggs, and vegetable oil with an electric mixer. Stir in grated apple. Fill cupcake liners ⅔ full.

Bake 18 minutes or until a toothpick inserted in the center comes out clean.

After you remove the cupcakes from the oven, poke holes across the tops of the warm cupcakes and pour about a tablespoon or so of caramel topping over the tops of each one. Let cupcakes cool completely.

While the cupcakes are cooling, make your frosting. In a bowl, beat butter, powdered sugar, and a splash of cider with an electric mixer. Add more cider if frosting is too thick or more sugar if it's too thin. Top cooled cupcakes with your frosting.

Chocolate Apple Pecan Cobbler

The cake mix sprinkled on top makes a cobbler-like texture for your dessert. Yummy! The caramel pieces are found in a package just like chocolate chips on the chocolate chip aisle. If you can't find them, you could substitute chocolate or butterscotch pieces.

INGREDIENTS

1 box chocolate cake mix, divided

1 tablespoon cinnamon, divided

$^3/_4$ cup water

$^1/_4$ cup butter, cold and chopped into pieces

$^1/_2$ cup pecans (optional)

1 cup caramel pieces
(sold on the chocolate chip aisle)

2 (21 ounce) cans apple pie filling

Vanilla ice cream, optional

Preheat oven to 375 degrees.

Grease a 9 x 13 baking dish. Set aside.

Mix 2 cups of your chocolate cake mix, half a tablespoon of cinnamon and water until smooth. Set aside. In a separate bowl, combine the remaining half tablespoon of cinnamon and the rest of your cake mix. Add in your butter and combine with a fork until crumbly. Stir in pecans and caramel pieces.

Spoon the apple pie filling into prepared baking dish. Drizzle the smooth chocolate cake batter on top of pie filling. Sprinkle your pecan mixture on top of everything.

Bake for about 30 minutes or until bubbly around the edges. Serve with ice cream.

Peanut Butter S'mores Bars

These gooey bars are such a hit with my friends and family.

INGREDIENTS

1 box yellow cake mix

½ cup vegetable oil

2 eggs

12 full-size Reese's Peanut Butter Cups (not the mini ones)

1 (13 ounce) jar marshmallow crème

Preheat oven to 350 degrees. Grease one 8 x 8 pan (for a 9 x 13 pan, double the recipe).

In a mixing bowl, combine cake mix, vegetable oil, and eggs with an electric mixer. Spread ⅔ of the mixture across the bottom of your pan.

Unwrap each peanut butter cup and place them across the bottom of your pan on top of your cake mixture.

Spread your marshmallow creme across the top of the peanut butter cups in your pan covering the whole thing (I use almost all of the 13 ounce but not quite all of it…Just spread it out until the pan has a nice marshmallow creme layer).

Take the remaining ⅓ of your cake batter and dot it across the top. It won't spread evenly across the top, so don't worry! Just drop it around and when it bakes, it will spread out.

Bake about 30 minutes or until the bars are brown around the edges. (The marshmallow creme will bake up big and fluffy but after the bars set out a while, it will deflate.)

Let the bars cool on the counter at least 2 hours before cutting into them and serving.

Chocolate Chip Pumpkin Bars

Chocolate and pumpkin go beautifully together. These bars are a little spicy, a little chocolaty and a whole lot of yummy.

INGREDIENTS

1 box chocolate cake mix

4 eggs

1 stick melted butter

4 cups powdered sugar

1 (8 ounce) package cream cheese, softened

1 cup canned pumpkin

1 tablespoon pumpkin pie spice (or cinnamon)

1 cup chocolate chips

Preheat oven to 350 degrees. Grease a 9 x 13 baking dish.

In a bowl, combine cake mix, 2 eggs, and melted butter. Spread batter in bottom of pan.

In a second bowl, beat with electric mixer powdered sugar, 2 more eggs, cream cheese, pumpkin, and pumpkin pie spice until smooth. Stir in chocolate chips. Spread on top of crust mixture.

Bake 35 to 40 minutes until edges are brown and center set (it will still be slightly wobbly in the middle).

Cool on counter 30 minutes, then refrigerate 2 hours or up to 2 days.

God has two dwellings;
one in heaven, and the
other in a meek and
thankful heart.

~Izaak Walton

NOVEMBER

DINNER

Enchilada Chili

Italian Chicken Noodle Soup

Chicken Parmesan
Sloppy Joes

Chicken à la King

BBQ Quesadillas

Mini BBQ Turkey
Meatloaves

Beefy Mac

Taco Pasta

Sausage and Vodka Pasta

Frito Pie Casserole

BREAKFAST

Sausage Breakfast Casserole

Pumpkin Cinnamon Rolls

DESSERT

Streusel-Topped Sweet Potato Pie

Pecan Pie Bars

Pumpkin Marshmallow Frozen Pie

Coconut Cream Pie

Rustic Cobbler

Gingerbread Pumpkin Trifle

Enchilada Chili

This meal is so good that I have actually made it twice in one week, which is so rare for me! It's great because it's a one-pot meal and comes together in minutes. This is the kind of supper I make on really busy nights. In less than 20 minutes, my family is eating a hearty and yummy meal. Go for it!

INGREDIENTS

1 pound ground beef (or ground turkey or chicken)

Drizzle of extra virgin olive oil

Pinch of salt and pepper

1 tablespoon chili powder

1 onion, chopped

1 (14 ounce) can Rotel tomatoes

1 (10 ounce) can or bottle enchilada sauce

1½ cups frozen corn

1 (15 ounce) can mild chili beans, not drained

Tortilla chips, shredded cheese, chopped green onion, sour cream to garnish

In a large pot over medium-high heat, brown the ground meat in a drizzle of olive oil with a pinch of salt and pepper. Once browned, stir in the chili powder and onion and sauté for a few minutes. Stir in the tomatoes, enchilada sauce, corn, and beans. Reduce the heat to low and cook for about 10 minutes.

Ladle the chili into bowls and garnish with your favorite toppings.

Italian Chicken Noodle Soup

To make a chicken noodle soup with a twist, I decided to make a yummy Italian-style chicken noodle soup. The result? Fabulous! Simple. Hearty. Warm. Comforting. A yummy version of chicken noodle soup your family will love!

INGREDIENTS

1 pound boneless, skinless chicken breasts, uncooked (frozen or thawed)

1 (28 ounce) can whole peeled tomatoes

1 cup chicken broth

3 tablespoons Italian seasoning

3 cups short-cut pasta (I use shells), uncooked

Parmesan cheese to garnish

Layer the chicken, tomatoes, broth, and Italian seasoning in a slow cooker. Cover and cook on low for 6 to 7 hours or on high for 3 to 4 hours.

About 30 minutes before you're ready to eat, shred the chicken right inside the slow cooker with two forks. Then break the whole tomatoes into pieces inside the slow cooker with a fork. Stir in the uncooked pasta shells. Cover, turn the heat to high, and cook for about 30 more minutes or until the pasta is tender.

Ladle the soup into bowls and garnish with Parmesan cheese.

Chicken Parmesan Sloppy Joes

This sloppy joe favorite has all the bells and whistles of Chicken Parmesan, but it's simple enough to make on a busy weeknight. Yum. Yum. And more yum. So simple, so fast, and so good. Happy eating!

INGREDIENTS

1 tablespoon extra virgin olive oil

1 pound cooked chicken, shredded

Pinch of salt and pepper

1 (8 ounce) can tomato sauce

1 (10 ounce) can tomato soup

1 tablespoon Italian seasoning

1 cup mozzarella cheese, shredded

1/2 cup Parmesan cheese, grated

Chopped basil to garnish

4 burger buns

Preheat the oven to 400 degrees.

Place foil on a baking sheet and lightly spray it with cooking spray for easy cleanup. Set aside.

In a skillet over medium-high heat, drizzle 1 tablespoon of olive oil. Add the cooked chicken and a nice pinch of salt and pepper. Stir in the tomato sauce, soup, and Italian seasoning. Reduce the heat to low and simmer for about 5 minutes.

Open the burger buns so you have 8 halves. Spoon a little chicken mixture across each one, then top with a little shredded mozzarella and Parmesan.

Pop the baking dish into the oven and bake for about 12 to 15 minutes or until the cheese is nice and melted and lightly browned. Remove the dish from the oven and garnish with a little basil.

Chicken à la King

Chicken à la King is such a simple little comfort food dish. It's like a pot pie or chicken and dumplings—just cozy food. You can be totally versatile on your carb choices. I like a traditional biscuit with mine, but you can use toast, cornbread, an English muffin—or be like my hubby and go without. This meal is a must on chilly weeknights.

INGREDIENTS

1½ pounds boneless, skinless chicken breasts, uncooked

½ onion, chopped

1 can cream of chicken soup

2 tablespoons flour

1 cup frozen peas

1 cup frozen corn

Pinch of salt and pepper

Biscuits (or bread of your choice for serving)

Layer the chicken, onion, soup, and flour in the slow cooker. Give it all a quick stir and then cover. Cook on low for 6 to 7 hours or on high for 3 to 4 hours.

About 30 minutes before you're ready to eat, shred the chicken right inside the slow cooker with two forks. Stir in the frozen peas and corn with a generous pinch of salt and pepper. Cover and cook on high for another 20 to 30 minutes.

Spoon the chicken mixture over the top of biscuits and serve.

BBQ Quesadillas

I discovered BBQ Quesadillas in a café inside our gym that sells sandwiches and such, and they were divine! Thus, I decided one day to whip up a batch myself and make life simpler. I use pulled pork, but brisket will work too. The key is the pickles. Seriously, the pickles make the whole thing. True love in a quesadilla.

INGREDIENTS

1½ pounds Andrea's Pulled Pork, shredded (see page 128).

½ red onion, chopped

1 cup pickle slices, drained and chopped

1 cup Monterey Jack cheese, shredded

Extra BBQ sauce

8 large flour tortillas (the "burrito" sized ones work best)

Preheat the indoor griddle or a big skillet to medium-high heat. Spray lightly with cooking spray.

Lay out the tortillas. Spread the pulled pork across the bottom half of each tortilla. Add onion, pickles, and cheese on top of the pork. Drizzle just a bit more BBQ sauce. Fold the top part down to cover the bottom portion.

Place one quesadilla in the skillet. Brown on both sides (about 4 minutes or so on each side). Remove it once it is browned and slice in half (to give you two quesadillas). Repeat with remaining tortillas.

Mini BBQ Turkey Meatloaves

If I made my mom's meatloaf recipe every night of the week, my husband wouldn't complain. Over the years I've tweaked it into meatballs, a sloppy joe, and even a burger because I'm always thinking of ways to mix and match his favorite dish. When I made a turkey version, my hubby and kiddos were all happy eaters. This recipe makes five mini meatloaves. (Add 30 minutes baking time to make one big loaf.)

INGREDIENTS

1 pound ground turkey

1 cup panko or breadcrumbs

2 eggs, beaten

6 to 8 green onions, chopped (reserve a few for garnish)

1 teaspoon salt

5 tablespoons Worcestershire sauce, divided

1 1/2 cups ketchup, divided

2/3 cup brown sugar

1 teaspoon mustard

Preheat the oven to 350 degrees.

Line a baking sheet with foil for easy cleanup and lightly spray with cooking spray. Set aside.

Mix the ground turkey, panko or breadcrumbs, eggs, green onions, salt, 3 tablespoons of Worcestershire sauce, and 1/2 cup ketchup in a bowl. Shape the mixture into 4 or 5 mini meatloaves and place them on the prepared baking sheet. Bake them in the oven for about 20 minutes.

While the meatloaves are baking, combine the remaining 2 tablespoons of Worcestershire sauce, 1 cup ketchup, the brown sugar, and the mustard in a bowl. Once 20 minutes is up, top each meatloaf with sauce and return them to the oven for 5 to 10 more minutes.

Remove from the oven, garnish with a few more green onions, and serve.

Beefy Mac

This is the ideal weeknight supper for busy families. A quick and hearty casserole served family style. I like to serve this alongside a big Caesar salad.

INGREDIENTS

1 pound elbow noodles

1 pound ground beef

1 onion, chopped

1 (1 ounce) packet of ranch dressing and seasoning mix

1 (10 ounce) can Rotel tomatoes

1 (6 ounce) can tomato paste

1 1/2 cups shredded Gruyere cheese (or cheddar!)

Extra virgin olive oil

Salt and pepper

Preheat oven to 400 degrees.

Bring a large pot of water up to a boil. Once boiling, drop pasta in and cook to al dente (about six minutes).

Meanwhile, in a large oven-safe skillet or cast iron pot, brown ground beef in a drizzle of olive oil with a pinch of salt and pepper. Once browned and crumbly, add in chopped onion with another little pinch of salt and pepper and brown about 4 minutes. Next, stir in ranch seasoning, Rotel tomatoes, and tomato paste.

Drain water from the pasta and add hot pasta to ground beef mixture. Stir to make sure everything is mixed together and then top with shredded cheese.

Pop pan into the oven and brown for about five minutes. If you don't have an oven-safe skillet or cast iron pot, transfer your mixture to a 9x13 baking dish prior to browning in the oven.

Remove from oven and serve immediately.

Taco Pasta

A pasta that tastes like a taco? Yes! I saw several of these types of recipes floating around Pinterest, so I thought I'd create my own. This recipe is really yummy and super simple to make. It would also make a great freezer meal or potluck dish.

INGREDIENTS

Few tablespoons extra virgin olive oil

1 pound ground beef (or ground chicken or turkey)

1 packet taco seasoning

3 ounces cream cheese

2 cups taco sauce (or salsa)

1 cup frozen corn

1 cup Cheddar cheese, shredded

1 cup Monterey Jack cheese, shredded

1 pound pasta, any kind

Green onions and/or sour cream to garnish

Preheat the oven to 400 degrees.

In a large skillet, add a few tablespoons olive oil over medium-high heat. Brown the ground beef until it's crumbly and cooked. Meanwhile, bring water in another large pot to a boil. Drop the pasta and cook to al dente (6 to 7 minutes). Drain and reserve.

Once the ground meat is browned, reduce the heat to low and stir in the taco seasoning and cream cheese. Cook until the cream cheese is melted and incorporated. Stir in the taco sauce, corn, and half of both cheeses. Add the hot pasta and toss it until incorporated.

Pour the mixture into an 8 x 8 baking dish. Top with remaining cheeses. Cover the dish with foil and bake for about 15 minutes. Remove the foil and bake for another 5 minutes. Remove the dish from oven and garnish the pasta with green onions and/or sour cream.

Sausage and Vodka Pasta

I'm constantly revamping spaghetti and meat sauce to please my pasta lovers. And because I love ordering a vodka sauce on my pasta at restaurants, I thought I'd make my own! Don't worry if you have little ones; the sauce simmers long enough to let the alcohol burn off, but it leaves behind a great depth of flavor.

INGREDIENTS

1 (16 ounce) box fettuccine or spaghetti noodles

1 pound sausage (I use Italian pork sausage)

1 tablespoon extra virgin olive oil

1 onion, chopped

Pinch of salt and pepper

1 cup vodka

1 (6 ounce) can tomato paste

1 (8 ounce) can tomato sauce

3 tablespoons half-and-half, cream, or milk

1 cup Parmesan cheese, grated (plus a little more for garnish)

Basil to garnish

Bring a large pot of water to a boil over medium-high heat and drop the pasta to cook until al dente (6 to 7 minutes).

Meanwhile, in a large skillet over medium-high heat, brown the sausage in 1 tablespoon olive oil. Once the sausage is browned and crumbly, stir in the onion along with a pinch of salt and pepper. Sauté the onion and sausage mixture over medium heat for 4 or 5 minutes. Slowly stir in the vodka and deglaze the pan (scrape the little bits off the bottom with a wooden spoon as you stir in the vodka with the sausage and onion). Reduce the heat to medium-low and stir in the tomato paste and tomato sauce. Simmer together for 8 to 10 minutes, stirring often.

After 8 to 10 minutes, stir in the half-and-half (or cream or milk) and Parmesan cheese. Drain the pasta and add the cooked pasta to the meat sauce. Stir to combine everything.

Portion the pasta onto plates and garnish with chopped basil and a little more Parmesan cheese.

Frito Pie Casserole

This is not one of those trick recipes full of hidden goodness like spinach, kale, carrots, and so on. This is one of those recipes you make when you just need to make people happy. Happy with a hearty casserole on a cold fall night, happy at a potluck, so happy that they quickly gobble it up. It's just so good. Trust me, you should make this.

INGREDIENTS

1 pound ground beef

1 onion, chopped

1 packet taco seasoning

1 bag Frito style chips

1 (15 ounce) can corn

1 (16 ounce) can chili with no beans

3 cups Cheddar cheese, shredded

Sour cream to garnish

Preheat the oven to 350 degrees.

Over medium-high heat, brown the ground beef in a skillet until it's crumbly. Add the onions and seasoning and sauté for a few minutes.

In a 9 x 13 dish, layer half the ingredients in this order: chips, corn, chili, seasoned meat, and cheese. Repeat so you have layered the ingredients twice.

Cover and bake for about 25 to 30 minutes or until bubbly and hot in the center. Garnish with sour cream.

Sausage Breakfast Casserole

My mother-in-law made me this breakfast casserole years ago and it's my go-to favorite. I love all breakfast casseroles but I continue to come back to this one because it's so simple. You make it the night before and bake it in the morning. And it's always, always, always delicious. Enjoy!

INGREDIENTS

1 package breakfast sausage

1 box Texas Toast croutons (I use the Caesar flavored ones)

6 eggs beaten

2 cups milk

1 can cream of mushroom soup

1 tablespoon mustard powder

2 cups cheddar cheese, divided

Brown sausage over medium-high heat until cooked through and crumbled. Meanwhile, combine eggs, milk, soup, mustard, and one cup cheese in a bowl. In a 9 x 13 pan, layer cooked sausage across bottom, then layer your box of croutons. Next, pour egg mixture over the crutons. Finally, top with remaining one cup cheese. Cover and refrigerate overnight.

The next morning, bake casserole uncovered in a 350 degree oven for one hour.

Pumpkin Cinnamon Rolls

Really and truly, such an easy little breakfast for busy mornings (or lazy mornings too!).

INGREDIENTS

1 (13 ounce) can pizza crust or can crescent rolls

1 cup sugar

1½ tablespoons pumpkin pie spice, divided

1 cup canned pumpkin (I use Libby's)

1 tablespoon vegetable oil

1 cup powdered sugar

1 teaspoon of milk

Preheat oven to 350 degrees. Cover a baking sheet in foil or parchment paper and lightly spray with cooking spray to prevent sticking. Set aside.

Roll out pizza crust on the counter to make a rectangle (it should make one automatically without your having to use a rolling pin).

In a small bowl, combine sugar and one tablespoon of pumpkin pie spice. Sprinkle half of the sugar mixture over pizza crust. Reserve the rest of this mixture.

In a second small bowl, combine cup pumpkin and remaining ½ tablespoon of pumpkin pie spice. Spread this mixture all over the crust.

Roll the pizza crust up into a long cylinder and press the seam down so that it's in a log. Taking a sharp knife, slice the log into 8 (1-inch) pieces and lay them out on prepared baking sheet.

Sprinkle the remaining cinnamon-sugar mixture over the tops of all of your cinnamon rolls. Bake about 15 minutes.

While they're baking, make glaze. In a small bowl, whisk together the vegetable oil, powdered sugar, and milk. Add more powdered sugar if glaze is too thin and more milk if it's too thick. Drizzle glaze over warm rolls and serve.

Streusel-Topped Sweet Potato Pie

This is a mixed-and-matched version of sweet potato casserole. If you're looking for a new pie recipe for Thanksgiving, I highly recommend you give this one a try! You will need 1¹/₂ cups of mashed and cooked sweet potatoes for this recipe. You can either bake up two sweet potatoes and use the filling or you can mash up some canned sweet potatoes, drained.

INGREDIENTS

For the pie:

1¹/₂ cups mashed sweet potatoes

¹/₂ cup brown sugar

1 (14 ounce) can sweetened condensed milk

3 eggs

¹/₂ tablespoon pumpkin pie spice

1 uncooked pie shell (either homemade or from the refrigerator section)

For the streusel:

¹/₄ cup brown sugar

2 tablespoons flour

2 tablespoons butter, slightly softened and cut into pieces

1 teaspoon cinnamon

¹/₂ cup pecan pieces

Preheat oven to 425 degrees.

In a large mixing bowl, beat with an electric mixer the first 5 ingredients until smooth. Pour mixture into pie shell and bake at 425 degrees for 15 minutes, then reduce heat to 350 degrees and bake another 20 minutes. Add streusel topping (see below) and bake another 15 minutes. Remove from oven and allow to cool at least 30 minutes before slicing and serving.

In a small bowl, combine all of the streusel ingredients. The consistency will be crumbly. When it's time, sprinkle the topping over the top of the pie and continue baking.

Pecan Pie Bars

Pecan Pie is a Thanksgiving tradition for our family. In fact, I would say that it's the pie that's gobbled up the fastest. Pecan Pie Bars give you the same great flavor without any need to fuss with the crust.

INGREDIENTS

1 box yellow cake mix

½ cup vegetable oil

2 eggs

1 stick (8 tablespoons) butter

1 cup brown sugar

⅓ cup light Karo Syrup

2 cups chopped pecans

Preheat oven to 350 degrees. Grease one 9 x 13 pan. In a mixing bowl, combine cake mix, vegetable oil, and eggs with an electric mixer. Spread batter over the bottom of your pan. Bake 15 minutes.

Meanwhile, in a saucepan over medium heat, melt your butter, brown sugar, and Karo syrup. Allow to simmer one minute before removing from heat. Immediately stir your chopped pecans into your butter mixture after it has simmered.

After 15 minutes, remove your pan from the oven and pour your hot pecan mixture over the top. Spread it out to cover. Pop the pan back in the oven and bake an additional 20 minutes.

Remove from oven and let stand at least 30 minutes before slicing into bars and serving.

Pumpkin Marshmallow Frozen Pie

Every year I create a pumpkin pie alternative (not that I don't love pumpkin pie—it's actually my very favorite!). I just like to offer a little twist for those who are looking for something slightly different. If you're like me and have several Thanksgiving Day desserts and sides to prepare, go ahead and make this one a few days in advance.

INGREDIENTS

1 (15 ounce) can pumpkin

1 (7 ounce) jar Marshmallow Fluff (or sometimes called Marshmallow Cream)

¼ cup brown sugar

¼ cup powdered sugar

1 tablespoon pumpkin pie spice

½ (12 ounce) container Cool Whip, thawed slightly (reserve the other half)

1 (9 inch) graham cracker crust

In a large mixing bowl, combine the first 6 ingredients with a spoon. Once combined, spoon the mixture into the prepared graham cracker crust. Freeze at least 4 hours before serving (you can freeze up to 48 hours if you like). Thaw just a bit before slicing and serving. Garnish with a little extra Cool Whip.

Coconut Cream Pie

Coconut Cream Pie is on every dessert table at every holiday party my family has. Maybe we see the fluffy coconut and it reminds us of snow? Maybe we're just so obsessed with coconut that we can't stand not to have it on one of the biggest days of the year? I toast my sweetened flaked coconut in a dry skillet, turning it continuously, for about five minutes.

INGREDIENTS

2 cups toasted coconut, divided

1¹/₂ cups half and half

1¹/₂ cups milk

2 eggs, lightly beaten

1 cup sugar

¹/₂ cup flour

1 teaspoon vanilla

1 (8 ounce) Cool Whip whipped topping

1 homemade or store-bought pie crust baked in a 9 inch pie plate

In a saucepan over medium-high heat, bring the half and half, milk, eggs, sugar and flour to a boil, stirring constantly. Once the mixture boils, remove from heat and immediately stir in the vanilla and one cup of toasted coconut. Pour this filling into your baked pie shell.

Cover and chill at least 5 hours (I usually do it overnight).

Once chilled, combine your whipped topping and remaining cup toasted coconut (reserving just a little for garnish) and spread on top of your pie. Sprinkle a little more coconut on top. Cut and serve.

When not enjoying, keep in the refrigerator.

Rustic Cobbler

I've made this with both blackberries and peaches. You could use apples, pears, cherries, mixed berries...mix and match away. This is seriously the most versatile little recipe—in fact, I bet you have all the ingredients in your pantry right now!

INGREDIENTS

3 cups frozen blackberries (or peaches or canned apple pie filling, etc.)

1 cup all-purpose flour

1 cup sugar

1 egg

³/₄ cup butter, melted

Preheat oven to 375 degrees.

   Place frozen berries across the bottom of a greased 8 x 8 baking dish. In a mixing bowl, combine flour, sugar, and egg with a wooden spoon until crumbly. Sprinkle flour mixture down over your berries. Pour melted butter over everything. Bake about 40 minutes or until browned and bubbly.

Gingerbread Pumpkin Trifle

Simple, pumpkin, and made in advance. All three things I look for in a Thanksgiving dessert! Don't get caught up in the layering—as long as you have all three layers, it doesn't matter in which order you do it. I don't put the final Cool Whip on top until I'm ready to serve because it's hard to cover and refrigerate with the Cool Whip sticking out on top.

INGREDIENTS

1 box gingerbread cake mix plus all ingredients to prepare it per package directions (can't find gingerbread, use a spice cake mix instead!)

1 (3.4 ounce) instant pumpkin pudding mix (use vanilla if you can't find pumpkin)

2 cups milk

1 (15 ounce) can pumpkin (I use Libby's)

1 tablespoon cinnamon

1 (16 ounce) container Cool Whip

Toffee Bar bits to garnish (I use the Heath Toffee Bits found on the chocolate chip aisle)

Prepare and bake cake per package directions.

Let the cake cool and then slice it into chunks.

In a mixing bowl, whisk together your dry pudding mix and milk for 2 minutes (it will thicken up a bit). Gently stir in your pumpkin and cinnamon.

In one large trifle bowl or individual dishes, layer pumpkin mix, Cool Whip, pieces of cake and repeat. Try to repeat. End with pumpkin on top. Cover and refrigerate at least 4 hours or even overnight. Right before you're ready to serve, top with a little more Cool Whip and garnish with toffee pieces.

I will honor Christmas in my heart,
and try to keep it all year.

~CHARLES DICKENS

DECEMBER

DINNER

Crunchy BBQ Brisket Tacos

Chicken Chile Verde

Boneless Pork Rib Tacos

Pomegranate Spinach
Chicken Tacos

Chicken and Broccoli Bites

Red Beans and Rice

Italian Style Chicken
and Waffles

Perfect Parmesan Pasta

Creamy Tomato Chicken Pasta

Pasta Fagioli

Beef Stroganoff Meatballs

BREAKFAST

Quick and Easy French Toast

Eggnog Monkey Bread

DESSERT

Peppermint Cocoa Krispies Treats

Chocolate Peppermint Macaroons

Reindeer Food

Oreo Christmas Bark

Gingerbread Cupcakes with Eggnog
Cream Cheese Frosting

Red Velvet Whoopie Pies

Crunchy BBQ Brisket Tacos

These tacos are really and truly delicious. And easy too! No turning on the oven. No stove top work. Just good eatin'. You'll come home from a busy day and your brisket will be all cooked up and tender in the slow cooker. You'll add a little BBQ sauce and a few garnishes and you'll be done! Such a simple supper!

INGREDIENTS

1 brisket, 2 to 3 pounds

Drizzle of extra virgin olive oil

Salt and pepper

2 cups salsa

½ to 1 cup water

1 to 2 cups BBQ sauce

6 to 8 crunchy taco shells

Chopped green onions and/or Monterey Jack cheese to garnish

Preheat a heavy skillet with olive oil over medium-high heat and brown the brisket for 4 to 5 minutes on each side. Make sure you salt and pepper each side. Transfer the brisket to a slow cooker and pour the salsa over the top. Pour a little water over everything until the brisket is mostly covered in the salsa and water. Cover and cook on low for 7 to 8 hours or on high for 4 to 5 hours.

About 20 minutes before you're ready to eat, remove the brisket and place it on a cutting board. Cover it with foil. This will allow the meat to rest and the juices to redistribute and keep it moist. Discard all the liquid in the slow cooker.

After the brisket has cooled about 10 minutes, slice and chop it into pieces and place those pieces into a bowl. Add BBQ sauce and coat everything. Use as much BBQ sauce as you think your family will love.

Stuff each taco shell with some brisket mixture. Garnish with some shredded cheese and/or chopped onions.

Chicken Chile Verde

I love this meal because it's so easy, but my kiddos love it because they're into tortillas, chicken, salsa, and guacamole (Texas kids for sure!). I don't want it too spicy, though, so I use a mild salsa verde (green salsa). The jalapeños will not be as spicy after cooking all day, but you can omit those if you think they're too hot for your family.

INGREDIENTS

1 pound boneless, skinless chicken breasts, uncooked (not frozen)

1 green bell pepper, chopped

1 small onion, chopped

1 jalapeño, seeded and chopped

2 (4 ounce) cans chopped green chilies

1 (1 ounce) packet taco seasoning or 2 tablespoons chili powder

1 (16 to 24 ounce) jar salsa verde (green salsa)

1 cup chicken stock or water

8 tortilla shells (I use whole wheat)

Guacamole as a side or to garnish

Monterey Jack or Cheddar cheese to garnish, shredded

Squeeze of fresh lime juice (optional)

In a slow cooker, combine the chicken, bell pepper, onion, jalapeño, both cans of green chilies, the taco seasoning or chili powder, salsa, and chicken stock or water. Cover and cook on low for 6 to 8 hours or on high for 3 to 4 hours.

When you're ready to serve, shred the chicken right inside the slow cooker with two forks.

Top each tortilla with a little bit of the chicken mixture, some fresh guacamole, and a little cheese, plus a squeeze of lime juice (optional).

Boneless Pork Rib Tacos

Boneless pork ribs are perhaps the easiest thing in the world to make. You throw them in, add two ingredients, and then don't think about them again for another 8 hours. Easy, easy, easy! I like to serve mine over flour tortillas with an extra drizzle of BBQ sauce and some chopped green onions.

INGREDIENTS

1½ pounds boneless pork ribs (ask your butcher!)

1 (18 ounce) bottle of your favorite BBQ sauce

1 (12 ounce) jar grape jelly

Flour tortillas, optional

Chopped green onions, optional

In your slow cooker, layer in your boneless pork ribs, bottle of BBQ sauce (reserve a little extra for garnish), and entire jar of grape jelly. Cover and cook on low 6 to 8 hours or on high 3 to 4 hours.

Remove ribs from slow cooker (discarding liquids), serve, and enjoy!

Pomegranate Spinach Chicken Tacos

Pomegranate seeds and December just go hand in hand. This little super food here has great flavor, nice crunch, and a fun bright color that can cheer up any cold and gray day. We eat these tacos with candied jalapeños, but if you can't find those, regular deli jalapeños will work just fine too! A little heat goes great with the pomegranate seeds.

INGREDIENTS

1 pound chicken breasts

4 cups chicken stock or water

2 tablespoons chili powder

Flour tortillas

Candied jalapeños

White Cheddar cheese, grated

1½ cups fresh pomegranate seeds

8 green onions, chopped

Place chicken breasts and stock in slow cooker. Cook on low 6 to 8 hours or high 3 to 4 hours. When ready to serve, remove chicken from slow cooker and place in a bowl. Take two forks and shred chicken. Stir in chili powder.

Take each tortilla and build your taco. Add candied jalapeños, white cheddar, pomegranate seeds, and green onions.

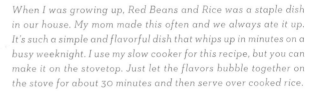

Chicken and Broccoli Bites

I love appetizers like this because they can also be quick lunches and light suppers! (Also, broccoli is my son's favorite vegetable, so I try to incorporate it into as many recipes as I can.) These little bites are so super simple to assemble, and they're delicious too. Enjoy!

INGREDIENTS

½ pound cooked and shredded chicken

1 (10 ounce) box frozen broccoli, thawed and drained of water

½ cup Swiss cheese, shredded

½ cup Cheddar cheese, shredded

1 (8 ounce) bottle ranch dressing

1 can refrigerated crescent rolls

Preheat the oven to 350 degrees.

Spray a cookie sheet with cooking spray or line it with parchment paper to prevent sticking. Set aside.

In a mixing bowl, combine the cooked chicken, broccoli, cheeses, and ranch dressing.

Unroll the crescent rolls and spoon about 2 tablespoons of the chicken filling in the center of each triangle. Fold the edges of the crescent roll over (like you normally would when making rolls) and place them on the cookie sheet.

Bake the Chicken and Broccoli Bites for about 10 to 12 minutes or until the rolls are lightly browned and the filling warm. Serve immediately.

Red Beans and Rice

When I was growing up, Red Beans and Rice was a staple dish in our house. My mom made this often and we always ate it up. It's such a simple and flavorful dish that whips up in minutes on a busy weeknight. I use my slow cooker for this recipe, but you can make it on the stovetop. Just let the flavors bubble together on the stove for about 30 minutes and then serve over cooked rice.

INGREDIENTS

1 pound uncooked sausage, sliced into round pieces or chopped (I use turkey sausage)

2 (15 ounce) cans red kidney beans, drained

1 (14 ounce) can diced tomatoes

1 onion, chopped

Hot pepper sauce to taste

Pinches of salt, pepper, and red pepper flakes to taste

2 cups cooked rice (I use brown rice)

Place the sausage, beans, tomatoes, and onion in the slow cooker. Add a few dashes of hot pepper sauce and a pinch of spices (you can always add more at the end if you need more flavor). Cover and cook on low for 6 to 8 hours or on high for 3 to 4 hours.

When you're ready to serve, ladle the mixture over the cooked rice.

Italian Style Chicken and Waffles

The name of this recipe might sound kind of fancy and daunting, but it's so easy. As soon as I made it, I started thinking of a million ways to mix and match! And if you use store-bought spaghetti sauce, you're really just assembling everything. This is such a yummy way to eat waffles for dinner. Enjoy!

INGREDIENTS

For the chicken:

1 pound chicken breasts

³/₄ cup Bisquick mix

2 tablespoons Italian seasoning

2 heaping tablespoons Parmesan cheese, finely grated

1 egg

2 tablespoons butter, melted

For the waffles:

4 cups Bisquick mix

2 cups milk

4 eggs

1 cup Parmesan cheese, grated

³/₄ cup chives, chopped

2 teaspoons black pepper

Spaghetti sauce

Preheat oven to 400 degrees. In one shallow dish (I use a pie plate), combine Bisquick, Italian seasoning, and cheese. In a second shallow dish, beat egg. Dip each chicken breast first in the Bisquick mix, coating well, and then dip it in the egg mix, coating both sides. Dip it one more time back in the Bisquick mix.

Place chicken on foil-lined cookie sheet sprayed with cooking spray. Brush half of your melted butter over the tops of the chicken and bake 8 minutes. Flip chicken over and brush remaining half of your melted butter on opposite side and finish cooking another 8 minutes. Your chicken should be brown and kind of crispy with the juices running clear.

Warm the spaghetti sauce and preheat the waffle iron. In a mixing bowl, combine the Bisquick mix, milk, and eggs to make the waffle batter. Stir in the cheese, chives, and pepper. Pour the batter into a hot waffle iron sprayed with cooking spray and bake until it's cooked through. This should make about 4 large waffles, depending on the waffle iron.

When the waffles are ready, top each waffle with chicken, then the sauce, and garnish with cheese and chives.

Perfect Parmesan Pasta

I call this Perfect Parmesan Pasta because it's like Chicken Parmesan but in a bowl with pasta. Basically, it's perfect. Your pasta lovers will totally dig this hearty supper.

INGREDIENTS

1 pound penne pasta

1 onion, chopped

3 cloves garlic, chopped

1 (28 ounce) can peeled tomatoes

1 (8 ounce) can tomato sauce

2 tablespoons Italian seasoning blend

1 pound cooked and shredded chicken (see page 6)

2 cups grated Mozzarella cheese

1 cup grated Parmesan cheese

Extra virgin olive oil

Salt and pepper

Preheat oven to 425 degrees. Grease an 8x8 baking dish and set aside.

Bring a large pot of water up to a boil. Drop in pasta and cook until al dente (about 7 to 8 minutes).

Meanwhile, in a large skillet over medium-high heat, heat a drizzle of olive oil and add in onion. Sauté until tender and then add garlic. Sauté another minute before adding in peeled tomatoes and tomato sauce. Break up peeled tomatoes with the back of a spoon. Stir in Italian seasoning and cooked and shredded chicken.

Drain pasta (reserve about a cup of the hot water). Add hot pasta and reserved water to skillet. Toss everything together and then pour it into prepared baking dish. Sprinkle cheese over the top of the casserole and pop it in the oven. Bake about 15 minutes or until the cheese is melted and bubbly.

Remove from oven and serve immediately.

Creamy Tomato Chicken Pasta

I'm always looking for new ways to make noodles, and this slow-cooker recipe is a good one! I think the key to a good slow-cooker meal is adding a little freshness at the end. The grated cheese and fresh basil really brighten up this meal. Also, I don't want the pasta to absorb all the sauce, so I cook up the pasta right before serving rather than cooking it in the slow cooker.

INGREDIENTS

1 pound boneless, skinless chicken breasts, uncooked (frozen or thawed)

1 cup chicken stock (or water)

1 (1 ounce) packet Italian dressing mix

1 onion, chopped

1 can tomato soup

1 (14 ounce) can diced tomatoes

4 ounces cream cheese

½ pound pasta, cooked (I use shells)

Parmesan cheese to garnish, grated

Fresh basil to garnish

In a slow cooker, combine the chicken, chicken stock, seasoning mix, onion, soup, and diced tomatoes. Cover and cook on low for 6 to 8 hours or on high for about 3 hours.

Thirty minutes before you're ready to serve, shred the chicken right inside the slow cooker with two forks. Turn the heat to high and add the cream cheese. Replace the lid and cook on high for another 30 minutes.

Right before you serve, add the hot, cooked pasta to the slow cooker and stir everything together.

Ladle the pasta into bowls and garnish with some grated Parmesan and fresh basil.

Pasta Fagioli

On dark and cold nights when you want to cuddle up with a yummy (and easy!) supper, this meal is for you. Hearty, simple, cozy, and delicious. I like to prepare my noodles on the stove top instead of adding them uncooked into the slow cooker so the noodles won't absorb the soup liquid. Also, if you substitute vegetable stock for the chicken stock, this is a vegetarian meal.

INGREDIENTS

1 (14 ounce) can diced tomatoes

1 (15 ounce) can Cannellini or Great Northern beans, rinsed and drained

1 (15 ounce) can kidney beans, rinsed and drained

1 (6 ounce) can tomato paste

2 tablespoons Italian seasoning

2 cups chicken stock

½ pound pasta, cooked (I use shells)

1 cup Parmesan cheese, grated

In a slow cooker, layer the first 6 ingredients (tomatoes through chicken stock). Cover and cook on low for 6 to 8 hours or on high for 3 to 4 hours. About 10 minutes before you're ready to serve, prepare the pasta. Combine the cooked pasta with the slow cooker ingredients at the end and stir.

Ladle the soup into bowls and top each bowl with grated Parmesan.

Beef Stroganoff Meatballs

Meatballs are a huge hit in our family, and don't all kids love pasta? When I whip up a meatball version of beef stroganoff to serve over noodles my family goes nuts. This meal is so simple and quick for those busy weeknights when you're trying to get dinner on the table.

INGREDIENTS

1 pound ground beef

½ onion, grated (use a cheese grater)

2 tablespoons Worcestershire sauce, divided

½ cup panko or breadcrumbs

2 eggs, lightly beaten

1 tablespoon butter

1 tablespoon flour

1 can cream of mushroom soup

2 cups chicken stock

1 teaspoon garlic powder

Pinch of salt and pepper

2 tablespoons sour cream (or more if you like)

½ pound cooked pasta for serving

Chopped green onions or scallions to garnish (optional)

Preheat the oven to 400 degrees.

Line a baking sheet with foil for easy cleanup and lightly spray with cooking spray. Set aside.

In a large mixing bowl, combine the ground beef, onion, 1 tablespoon of Worcestershire sauce, panko or breadcrumbs, and eggs. Form small meatballs (I make 18, but you might make more or less depending on the size you roll yours). Place the meatballs on the prepared baking sheet and roast for about 15 minutes or until browned.

While the meatballs are roasting, heat 1 tablespoon butter over medium-high heat in a large skillet. Quickly whisk the flour into the melted butter and whisk for about a minute. Stir in the soup, the remaining tablespoon of Worcestershire sauce, and the chicken stock, and bring to a little bubble. Then reduce the heat to low. Stir in the garlic powder and a nice pinch of salt and pepper.

Remove the meatballs from the oven and add them to your skillet mixture to simmer for about 10 minutes, stirring often. Right before serving, stir in the sour cream.

Serve the meatballs and some sauce over cooked noodles. Garnish with chopped green onions or scallions (optional).

Quick and Easy French Toast

My version can easily be doubled for larger families, but for us, we use half a whole grain French baguette which produces 5 nice, thick slices. You can use any kind of bread you like (our bakery just makes an amazing whole grain baguette). You can use a regular French baguette, thick slices of sandwich bread, or challah.

INGREDIENTS

1 French baguette (or the bread of your choice), about 5 or 6 slices

2 eggs, lightly beaten

1½ cups milk

2 teaspoons vanilla extract

½ cup chocolate chips

½ cup butterscotch chips

1 cup slivered almonds

Maple syrup to garnish

Preheat your griddle or a large non-stick pan to medium-high heat.

In a large mixing bowl, beat your eggs and milk together with a whisk. Whisk in vanilla. Dip each slice of bread in egg mixture and place it in your hot skillet. Brown each side about two minutes before flipping. Once browned on both sides, remove to serving plate and sprinkle chocolate and butterscotch chips over the top along with slivered almonds. Drizzle syrup over the top.

Eggnog Monkey Bread

Every Christmas morning should have a simple and yummy make-ahead breakfast to enjoy with present opening and coffee! Now, I use eggnog for the glaze but if that's not your thing, substitute milk instead.

INGREDIENTS

½ cup sugar

1 tablespoon cinnamon

3 (16.3 ounce) cans refrigerated flaky layer biscuit dough, cut into quarters

¾ cup firmly packed brown sugar

½ cup butter

¼ cup light corn syrup

3 tablespoons eggnog (or milk)

1 cup powdered sugar

Preheat oven to 350 degrees. Spray a Bundt pan with cooking spray.

In a small bowl, combine sugar and cinnamon. Dredge biscuit quarters in sugar mixture to coat. Layer in prepared pan. (At this point, you can cover and refrigerate this until the next morning.)

In a small saucepan, combine brown sugar, butter, and corn syrup. Cook over medium-high heat stirring constantly until mixture comes to a boil. Boil one minute. Pour over layered biscuits. Bake 40 minutes. Let pan sit 5 minutes before inverting it onto platter to serve.

To make your glaze, combine eggnog (or milk) in a small bowl with your powdered sugar. Add more eggnog if the glaze is too thick and more powdered sugar if it's too thin. Pour glaze over warm monkey bread and serve.

Peppermint Cocoa Krispies Treats

Simple, festive, quick, delicious, cocoa, Christmas.

INGREDIENTS

3 tablespoons butter

4 cups mini marshmallows

6 cups Cocoa Krispies cereal

1 cup peppermint crunch

Over medium heat, melt butter in sauce pan. Add in marshmallows, stirring until melted. Pour over cereal. Stir in the peppermint crunch. Mix well and then spread in a greased 8 x 8 baking dish. (Spray a spatula with cooking spray and press it over the top to get the cereal to stay put in the baking dish.)

Cut into squares and enjoy!

Chocolate Peppermint Macaroons

Be still my heart. These might actually be my absolute favorite thing I make. Period. These little bites of goodness look fancy and are perfect for a little holiday fete but trust me . . . they are so simple. Really and truly so, so, so simple. This Christmas season, whether you're hosting a little something yourself, asked to bring something to a party, or just want something a little extra special while watching A Christmas Story one night, you should make these.

INGREDIENTS

5½ cups sweetened flaked coconut

⅓ cup all-purpose flour

½ teaspoon salt

1 (14 ounce) can sweetened condensed milk

1 teaspoon vanilla

8 ounces chocolate almond bark

1 teaspoon peppermint extract

about one cup peppermint crunch

Preheat your oven to 350 degrees. Spray your cookie sheet with cooking spray or line it with parchment paper. Set aside.

In a mixing bowl, combine coconut and flour with a wooden spoon. Stir in your salt, milk, and vanilla. Drop by 2 tablespoons onto your parchment paper.

Bake 15 to 20 minutes or until lightly brown and toasted. Remove from oven to cool 1 minute while you're preparing the chocolate.

Microwave the almond bark, stirring every 45 seconds until smooth. Immediately stir in the peppermint extract. Drizzle your chocolate peppermint over each macaroon and then go back and quickly sprinkle the peppermint crunch on top (the chocolate will set quickly).

Serve either warm or room temp. Store in an airtight container on the counter.

Reindeer Food

This time of year, I always like having sweet treats like this around the house to munch on. It's so fun to sit down with Christmas Vacation and have a little Christmas goodie to eat. I also think recipes like this make the perfect little gift to share with neighbors, coworkers, teachers, and friends. Plus, this is one of those really fun activities to do in the kitchen with young kiddos!

INGREDIENTS

1 bag of popped popcorn (about 4 cups total)

4 cups Rice Chex cereal

8 ounces white candy coating or almond bark

1 (9 ounce) bag Peppermint M&Ms

1 (9 ounce) bag milk chocolate red and green M&Ms

2 cups peppermint crunch

Red sprinkles

Lay wax paper down over your kitchen counters to pour your Reindeer Food on.

In a large mixing bowl, combine your popcorn and Chex cereal together.

In a microwavable bowl, melt your candy coating, stirring every 45 seconds. Once it's melted, quickly pour it over your popcorn mixture and toss. Working quickly, add in M&Ms, Peppermint Crunch, and sprinkles and then pour the mixture onto the wax paper to dry (about 10 minutes). Once it's dried, store in an airtight container.

And of course, you could mix and match this a million ways by adding in your favorite Christmas candy!

Oreo Christmas Bark

You know how I love making bark. It's the easiest candy in the world and the ultimate mix and match recipe. The best part? You can't screw it up. Add whatever Christmas candy makes you happy. This will last weeks in the fridge or freezer. The perfect party snack or gift for a friend or neighbor.

INGREDIENTS

1 package white chocolate candy coating

10 Christmas Oreos, crushed

¼ cup pretzel sticks, broken into pieces

Christmas M&Ms

A few tablespoons peppermint crunch

Christmas sprinkles

A handful of white chocolate chips and/or mint chocolate chips

In a microwavable bowl, melt white chocolate coating (stopping to stir every 45 seconds). Once melted, pour onto a cookie sheet lined with wax paper. Immediately, top with cookies, pretzels, sprinkles, and candy and slightly press into chocolate (I use a large spatula to press the candy into the chocolate). Refrigerate at least one hour. Pull from fridge, break into pieces with your hands.

Gingerbread Cupcakes with Eggnog Cream Cheese Frosting

Instead of making another batch of gingerbread men this year... why don't you try one of these yummy cupcakes? Topped with a seasonal frosting, they are a crowd pleaser and new holiday favorite at our house. As for the eggnog in the frosting, you can either use homemade or buy a bottle from the grocery store (next to the other dairy products this time of year).

INGREDIENTS

1²⁄₃ cups flour	1 egg
1 tablespoon ground ginger	½ cup boiling water
2 teaspoons pumpkin pie spice	1 (8 ounce) package cream cheese, softened
1 teaspoon baking soda	2 cups powdered sugar
½ cup sugar	2 to 3 tablespoons prepared eggnog
½ cup molasses	A little cinnamon, pumpkin pie spice, or nutmeg to garnish
½ cup vegetable oil	

Preheat oven to 350 degrees. Fill 2 (12 count) muffin tins with cupcake liners (you'll probably only fill 18 of them).

In a large mixing bowl, combine flour, ginger, pumpkin pie spice, and baking soda with a whisk. In a second bowl, beat with an electric mixer the sugar, molasses, oil, and egg until combined. Slowly beat the sugar mixture into the flour mixture. Pour boiling water over the top of the batter and beat until it's combined.

Fill your cupcake liners with batter. Bake about 8 minutes or until a toothpick inserted into the middle comes out clean. Allow cupcakes to cool completely before frosting.

To make the frosting, beat the cream cheese, powdered sugar, and eggnog with an electric mixer until smooth. Add more eggnog if the frosting is too thick and more sugar if it's too thin. Frost cupcakes and garnish with a little sprinkle of spice. When not enjoying, store in the refrigerator.

Red Velvet Whoopie Pies

A festive dessert for a festive season. Oh, and by the way, they have a chocolate chip cream cheese filling. Yes. I went there.

INGREDIENTS

1 box red velvet cake mix	1/4 cup water
1/2 cup vegetable oil	Store-bought cream cheese frosting
2 eggs	1/2 cup mini chocolate chips

Preheat oven to 350 degrees. Combine cake mix, oil, eggs, and water in bowl. Drop by 2 tablespoons onto lined cookie sheet (leave about an inch between each cookie). Bake 9 to 10 minutes. Cool on pan 5 minutes, move to wire rack, and cool 15 more minutes.

Pour frosting into a bowl. Add in chocolate chips and stir until chips are evenly distributed in frosting. Take one cookie and place a tablespoon or so of frosting in the center. Press another cookie on top (this will spread the frosting out to the edge).

ACKNOWLEDGMENTS

This book would not have been possible without the love and support of my sweet family and friends. Growing up, I had two amazing grandmothers and one precious mama who taught me the value in cooking for family. Time spent at the table and in the kitchen shaped me into the woman I am today.

Thank you to my sweet girlfriends who talk food with me endlessly. Thank you for always humoring me when I grill you on what you're having for dinner. Your dedication to your own families and mealtimes with them motivates and encourages me daily.

Thank you to my beloved Sunday school class... otherwise known as my taste-testers. You guys have been eating my food and reporting back to me for more than four years now! Your honest input, opinions, and enthusiasm make it so much fun to bring you food every week. I love sharing these recipes with all of you!

This book wouldn't be here without the encouragement and support of my agent, Ruth Samsel, and the amazing team at Harvest House. Thank you all for always encouraging me to put my family first and foremost. Thank you especially to Kathleen Kerr and Heather Green, who read my mind and know my heart. I'm blessed to work with all of you.

To my sweet blog readers who come back day after day to read my words and see my recipes . . . from the bottom of my heart, thank you. Your support and love over the last eight years have spoken into my life more than you'll ever know. I am eternally grateful for each of you and thankful that you invite me into your homes each day. God bless you all.

Andrew, Kensington, Smith, and Ashby . . . you are my world. I am honored to be a member of this precious family, and my greatest legacy is you.

Without my faith in Jesus Christ, I would not be the person I am today . . . born a sinner, saved by grace. You are my joy, my peace, my hope . . . my everything.

RECIPE INDEX

With Meals This Easy to Make, There's *Always* Time for Cake

Want even more delicious dinner and dessert ideas from Shay?
Get these two amazing books and discover what else the Mix-and-Match Mama eats.

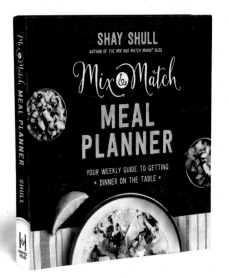

Turn Shay's tastiest recipes into easy weekly meal plans with the **Mix-and-Match Meal Planner,** with bonus content such as helpful shopping and pantry essentials lists, tips and tricks for streamlining your cooking, and dozens of great ideas to help you make dinner fun for the whole family.

Loved the dessert recipes in *Mix-and-Mama Eats* and want more? Get all of Shay's 101 tasty cake recipes in one helpful collection. **Mix-and-Match Cakes** will help you discover the simple secret to delicious, "wow-worthy" cakes that will have your family and friends begging for your recipe. You'll be inspired to make every day a little sweeter.

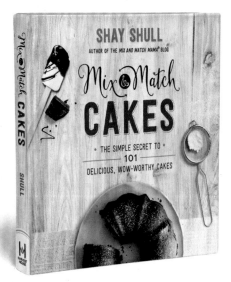

DINNER? DESSERT? DONE!
IT'S THAT SIMPLE!